THE HAMLYN LECTURES

TWENTY-FIFTH SERIES

MALADMINISTRATION AND ITS REMEDIES

AUSTRALIA
The Law Book Company Ltd.
Sydney : Melbourne : Brisbane

CANADA AND U.S.A.
The Carswell Company Ltd.
Agincourt, Ontario

INDIA
N. M. Tripathi Private Ltd.
Bombay

ISRAEL
Steimatzky's Agency Ltd.
Jerusalem : Tel Aviv : Haifa

MALAYSIA : SINGAPORE : BRUNEI
Malayan Law Journal (Pte) Ltd.
Singapore

NEW ZEALAND
Sweet & Maxwell (N.Z.) Ltd.
Wellington

PAKISTAN
Pakistan Law House
Karachi

MALADMINISTRATION AND ITS REMEDIES

BY

K. C. WHEARE
Fellow of All Souls College, Oxford

Published under the auspices of
THE HAMLYN TRUST

LONDON
STEVENS & SONS
1973

Published in 1973
by Stevens & Sons Limited
of 11 New Fetter Lane in
the City of London and
printed in Great Britain by
The Eastern Press Limited
of London and Reading

SBN Hardback 0420 44320 7
Paperback 420 44330 4

CONTENTS

THE HAMLYN LECTURES

1949 Freedom under the Law
by The Rt. Hon. Lord Denning

1950 The Inheritance of the Common Law
by Richard O'Sullivan, Esq.

1951 The Rational Strength of English Law
by Professor F. H. Lawson

1952 English Law and the Moral Law
by Dr. A. L. Goodhart

1953 The Queen's Peace
by Sir Carleton Kemp Allen

1954 Executive Discretion and Judicial Control
by Professor C. J. Hamson

1955 The Proof of Guilt
by Dr. Glanville Williams

1956 Trial by Jury
by The Rt. Hon. Lord Devlin

1957 Protection from Power under English Law
by The Rt. Hon. Lord MacDermott

1958 The Sanctity of Contracts in English Law
by Sir David Hughes Parry

1959 Judge and Jurist in the Reign of Victoria
by C. H. S. Fifoot, Esq.

1960 The Common Law in India
by M. C. Setalvad, Esq.

1961 British Justice: The Scottish Contribution
by Professor T. B. Smith

THE HAMLYN TRUST

The Hamlyn Trust came into existence under the will of the late Miss Emma Warburton Hamlyn of Torquay, who died in 1941 at the age of eighty. She came of an old and well-known Devon family. Her father, William Bussell Hamlyn, practised in Torquay as a solicitor for many years. She was a woman of strong character, intelligent and cultured, well versed in literature, music and art, and a lover of her country. She inherited a taste for law, and studied the subject. She also travelled frequently on the Continent and about the Mediterranean, and gathered impressions of comparative jurisprudence and ethnology.

Miss Hamlyn bequeathed the residue of her estate in terms which were thought vague. The matter was taken to the Chancery Division of the High Court, which on November 29, 1948, approved a Scheme for the administration of the Trust. Paragraph 3 of the Scheme is as follows:—

> "The object of the charity is the furtherance by lectures or otherwise among the Common People of the United Kingdom of Great Britain and Northern Ireland of the knowledge of the Comparative Jurisprudence and the Ethnology of the chief European countries including the United Kingdom, and the circumstances of the growth of such jurisprudence to the intent that the Common People of the United Kingdom may realise the privileges which in law and custom they enjoy in comparison with other European Peoples and realising and appreciating such privileges may recognise the responsibilities and obligations attaching to them."

From the first the Trustees decided to organise courses of lectures of outstanding interest and quality by persons of eminence, under the auspices of co-operating universities or other bodies, with a view to the lectures being made available in book form to a wide public.

The Twenty-Fifth Series of Hamlyn Lectures was delivered in November 1973 by Sir Kenneth Wheare at Southampton.

J. N. D. ANDERSON,
Chairman of the Trustees.

November 1973

CHAPTER 1

MALADMINISTRATION

I

ONE of the aims of the Hamlyn lectures is " that the common people of the United Kingdom may realise the privileges which in law and custom they enjoy in comparison with other European peoples. . . ." There is, as you see, a large assumption of superiority built in here. I have chosen maladministration and its remedies as the field in which to test and illustrate this assumption. Maladministration is a very large subject; it occurs wherever social organisation exists. It is not confined to the operations of the government or the state alone. But I shall confine myself in these lectures to a discussion of maladministration as it occurs in the course of actions by the officials of government, central and local, in Britain. And I shall confine myself still further by considering chiefly the working of certain institutions through which it is intended that maladministration should be remedied. I shall consider how adequate they are, and how they compare, in effectiveness and scope, with some of those available to citizens in some other countries, in Europe or in the Commonwealth or in the United States. In speaking of " remedies," I will take advantage of the fact that I am not a lawyer but only a political scientist, and will use the term in a wider and looser sense than is normally employed by an administrative lawyer. Although legal remedies, strictly so called, form part of my exposition, I shall regard a question in Parliament, a tribunal of inquiry, a select committee of the House of Commons, for example, as among the institutions for providing remedies for maladministration as much as an order of mandamus or certiorari or an injunction from the High Court.

I must concede, of course, that the whole subject of the prevention and cure of maladministration by government officials embraces and involves consideration of a far wider field than that of remedies designed to put right an act of maladministration after it has occurred. It opens up the great questions of how a civil service should be recruited, trained, and organised so that it can be capable of providing good administration and thereby avoiding maladministration. Some would say that this positive approach is the better way of reducing or eliminating maladministration. Should not the emphasis be placed on prevention in advance rather than in providing institutions designed to come into action after a mistake has been made? Ought we not to seek the principles of good administration and embody them in the organisation and training of civil servants, rather than to identify cases of maladministration and their appropriate remedies? It was with this sort of approach that the Fulton Committee on the Civil Service [1] was concerned, and it may be presumed that such questions are the continuing concern of the Civil Service Department, whose political head is the Prime Minister, and of the Civil Service College.

The topic of remedies is, therefore, only a small part of this bigger subject of how to ensure good government. But although it is small, it is important, and, I would say, likely

[1] The Committee, under the chairmanship of Lord Fulton, sat from 1966–68. Its task was "to examine the structure, recruitment and management, including training, of the Home Civil Service and to make recommendations." Its report is Cmnd. 3638.

to become of increasing importance. Although a lot has been talked and written about it in recent years, it would be a mistake to think that there is no cause for concern. Indeed the more "efficient" administration becomes as a result of the activities of such bodies as the Fulton Committee, the more anxiety must we feel about the position of the ordinary citizen who thinks that he has suffered injustice at the hands of the well-organised machine. In simple words, there is a very great deal of administration by government officials going on and it is certain that there will be a great deal more. It is not eccentric to conclude that if there is more administration, there will be more maladministration.

Some recent developments in the governmental system in Britain may illustrate the position. By the Local Government Act of 1972, the areas of local government in England have been considerably enlarged in size while the number of authorities has been reduced. One certain result of this is that the centres where official power is exercised will be more remote from many citizens than they were before. The setting up of this new structure of local government has been accompanied by a belief that, irrespective of questions of area, a greater freedom should be given to officials in local authorities to exercise power uncontrolled in detail by local councillors. This was a leading theme in the Report of the Committee on the Management of Local Government in England and Wales under the chairmanship of Sir John Maud (later Lord Redcliffe-Maud) which published its report in 1967. It compared English practice unfavourably with that of foreign countries where local authorities delegated much more power to take decisions to the officers than was the practice in England, and it recommended that this principle should be introduced into the English authorities.[2] Their creed is well illustrated in a significant paragraph: "The idea that English local government is peculiarly democratic originates in the participation of members in so much detail. For, unlike the members abroad, they believe, mistakenly in our opinion, that democratic government implies that to discharge their duties, they must leave as little as possible to the officers."[3] And they recommended that, while council members must exercise sovereign power within the authority and accept responsibility for everything done in the council's name, they must, having settled the policy, delegate to officers the taking of all but the most important decisions.[4] Thus, we can now have more administration by officials, and by officials more remote from the citizens than formerly. In this new order for local government, whatever its advantages, the problem of maladministration and its remedies does not become less.

When we look at recent trends in the organisation of central government in Britain similar misgivings arise. One such trend is the setting up of what are called the "giant" departments—the Foreign and Commonwealth Office, the Ministry of Defence, the Department of Trade and Industry, the Department of the Environment and the Department of Health and Social Security are examples.[5] When we read[6] of the Department of Trade and Industry that in 1971 it had a staff of 26,000 people (excluding industrial staff), a

2 Report, Vol. 1, Chaps. 2 and 3, esp. paras. 57–73 and 151.
3 Para. 40.
4 p. x.
5 See *The Reorganisation of Central Government*, a White Paper issued in October 1970. Cmnd. 4506.
6 In the Report of the Tribunal of Inquiry into the cessation of trading by the Vehicle and General Insurance Co. Ltd., H.C. 133 of 1971–72, paras. 62 and 63.

permanent secretary, two second permanent secretaries, seventy under-secretaries, and thereunder numerous assistant secretaries, and that it was organised on the basis that almost all the work allotted to the various divisions of the Department should be dealt with fully and finally at the level of under-secretary or below, we are bound to think that the Secretary of State for the Department and the two or three Ministers within the Department subordinate to him must be very detached from ordinary administration or maladministration. It is not surprising to read also that the proportion of the work of the Department that is referred to Ministers is very small—well under 1 per cent.[7] We compare these figures with those of the Board of Trade (an ingredient of the new giant) which, ten years earlier, employed 7,000 people (non-industrial) and was staffed by seventeen under-secretaries. If this vogue for giant Ministries continues, the delegation of authority and responsibility to officers, only very remotely and intermittently controlled by Ministers, is bound to establish itself. Among the many problems which the institution of the " giants " brings—and it is not implied that those responsible for the organisation of the machinery of government and the efficiency of the officials are unaware of them [8]—one at least is obvious—how remedies against maladministration may be made effective in such an official structure.

In thinking about the governmental system of the United Kingdom in these days, we must include the institutions of the European Economic Community in our consideration. At their present stage, it is clear that their leading charac-

[7] Para. 61.
[8] See Sir Richard Clarke's lectures to the Civil Service College, *New Trends in Government*, H.M.S.O., 1971.

teristic is the predominant power of officials, subject to what seems, from the outside at least, a very minimum of control. In so far as their decisions operate within the United Kingdom, there is created a new and important area of government by officials with a possibility (to say the least) of maladministration for which appropriate remedies are by no means obvious.

II

" Nobody can define maladministration in plain terms," said Sir Edmund Compton, the first British Parliamentary Commissioner for Administration or Ombudsman.[9] It may be difficult to define, but most of us believe that we could recognise an example of it, if we saw it. We can describe it by examples. We know what it is, but we are quite ready to admit that we might find ourselves in disagreement with other people about whether or not a particular case was an example of maladministration. We would admit also that there might be a vague and uncertain boundary surrounding the areas of maladministration.

In a sense it all comes back to what you mean by " administration " itself. If you include within it a measure of rule-making and of adjudication, you widen the notion of administration and in so doing the area in which maladministration can occur. If on the other hand you give the word a narrower meaning, and in particular exclude rule-making and adjudication, the meaning of maladministration is correspondingly confined. These are important questions, as we shall see, and not only for political and constitutional

[9] In answer to a question by a member of the Select Committee on the Parliamentary Commissioner for Administration in 1968. H.C. 350 of 1967–68, Minutes of Evidence, Qu. 151.

theory.[10] For the present I will say that I intend to use the term " administration " in the wider sense. After all, the making of statutory orders, to take an example, is one of the ways in which departments administer Acts of Parliament, and is, in that sense, part of the administrative process.[11] It is true that there are difficult arguments about where the line is to be drawn, but it seems to me that to confine the meaning of administration narrowly is to condemn oneself to an unrealistic and unfruitful approach to the study of the subject.

Let us see where we get by quoting some examples. There is little doubt that we would all regard official action which transgressed the law as an example of maladministration. This could arise, say, from a failure to carry out a duty imposed by law, or from action which went beyond the powers conferred by law or used the power conferred by law for a purpose for which it was not intended. It could arise from action which did not follow a procedure laid down by law, whether by statute or by the courts in various decisions designed to prevent, so far as possible, the making of arbitrary or unreasonable decisions in the application of legal powers.

We would also regard as falling within the scope of maladministration actions which were influenced by what is loosely described as bribery and corruption. In most cases this would amount to a form of illegality, but there can be examples where influence may be used to persuade officials either to act or not to act in an area where they have discretion but where, though it might not be clear that

[10] Some notion of the importance and complexity of the question is gained from Geoffrey Marshall's article " Maladministration " in [1973] P.L. 32.

[11] H.C. 350 of 1967–68, p. 91, Sir Edmund Compton.

illegality was involved, it could be urged that maladministration had occurred. In Britain it is almost taken for granted that maladministration of this kind not only should not occur but rarely does occur among the officials of the central government. There may not be the same degree of certainty where local government is concerned. On the whole, however, it is generally thought that this kind of corrupt behaviour is a characteristic of foreign countries and foreign officials rather than of British. But it is worth pausing for a moment to record that it is a remarkable situation, if true.

Yet there is still a wide area of possible maladministration, even if we put aside actions which are illegal or near criminal or financially corrupt. After all, while " incorruptibility and efficiency are two obvious requirements for public confidence in the administration of government departments " [12] " the citizen has a right to expect not only that his affairs will be dealt with effectively and expeditiously, but also that his personal feelings no less than his rights as an individual will be sympathetically and fairly considered." [13] These words, from the report of a committee set up after the Crichel Down affair and of which a distinguished civil servant, Sir John Woods, was chairman, indicate in some way the width of the concept of maladministration and stress the necessity of extending one's view beyond questions of illegality, essential as they are.

The ordinary citizen in his dealing with officials, whether central or local, is engaged as a rule in small matters, important to him but run of the mill to the official. In this

[12] Quoted in the debate on the Crichel Down affair in the House of Commons on July 20, 1954. H.C.Deb., Vol. 530, 5 s., cols. 1240–1241.
[13] *Ibid.*, col. 1288.

area he can encounter, on occasion, delay, discourtesy, unfairness, bias, ignorance, incompetence and high-handedness. Ordinary mistakes, the result of ordinary human error, can be made by officials in dealing, for example, with pensions, allowances, taxes, rates, social assistance and welfare, in applying the mass of detailed regulations to the particular cases. All this can happen and can be admitted to happen without any imputations against officials of extraordinary incompetence or ill will. Nor should they be thought of as examples of maladministration which are confined to or peculiar to government offices. Those who deal with any organisation, especially any large organisation, such as a bank or an insurance company or a chain store or a supermarket will have experienced, most often perhaps at the counter (which is as far as the ordinary citizen usually gets), occasions of delay, discourtesy, ignorance, incompetence, rudeness and the rest, and will have been left with a feeling of impotence in attempting to find a remedy for acts of maladministration against these anonymous, remote, and impersonal mammoths.

In the Act setting up the British Ombudsman—the Parliamentary Commissioner for Administration Act 1967 [14] —the expression " maladministration " was used, but no definition or explanation of it was embodied in the Act. In moving the second reading of the Bill in the House of Commons, Mr. Crossman, Lord President of the Council in the Labour Government of Mr. Harold Wilson, while defending the decision not to define " maladministration," declared that " it would be a wonderful exercise " to try—" bias, neglect, inattention, delay, incompetence, ineptitude,

[14] 1967, c. 13.

perversity, turpitude, arbitrariness and so on. It would be a long and interesting list."[15]

And in the course of reviewing the first year's operation of the Act, the select committee of the House of Commons associated with the Parliamentary Commissioner's work, heard a list of examples of maladministration from the lips of the Head of the Home Civil Service, Sir William Armstrong: failure to answer a letter; losing the papers or part of them; giving misleading statements to citizens about their legal position; delay in reaching a decision; exhibiting bias; giving incomplete or ambiguous instructions to the officer who is applying the rule; getting the facts of the case wrong; or failing to take facts into account which the department should have taken into account.[16]

In the pursuit of maladministration, concepts of misconduct and negligence have been introduced into the discussion. I content myself, at this stage, with quoting a passage from the report of a tribunal of inquiry in which these concepts were applied in judging the performance of civil servants. "Misconduct has many shades of meaning. . . . We construe 'misconduct' as a deliberate dereliction of duty on the part of a person who knows that he is acting wrongfully and in breach of duty."[17] "The relevant concept of negligence is a departure from the required standard of competence, whether it be by action or by failure to take action, though not every departure is necessarily negligence."[18] "We apply this test: is it shown, quite clearly, that there was a departure from the ordinary competence of a reasonable person exercising this particular

[15] October 18, 1966, H.C.Deb., Vol. 734, 5 s., col. 51.
[16] H.C. 350 of 1967–68, pp. 100–101, Qu. 643.
[17] H.C. 133 of 1971–72, para. 316.
[18] Para. 320.

skill to such an extent that the departure must be regarded, in common sense, as deserving condemnation beyond criticism? If so, and only if so, is negligence established in the present context." [19] The question may be clear; the answer must be very difficult!

To continue with these examples of examples may confirm the suspicion that we are engaged in filling a rag bag. In the chapters that follow we shall be discussing many cases and forms of alleged maladministration. It will suffice now to sum up with a short statement which epitomises, in fairly general terms, a good deal of what has been said already. Maladministration may be described as "administrative action (or inaction) based on or influenced by improper considerations or conduct. Arbitrariness, malice or bias, including discrimination, are examples of improper considerations. Neglect, unjustifiable delay, failure to observe relevant rules and procedures, failure to take relevant considerations into account, failure to establish or review procedures where there is a duty or obligation on a body to do so, are examples of improper conduct." [20]

May I add one footnote to this discussion. It is sometimes assumed that in identifying maladministration, we cannot question the rules, only the actions of those who are applying the rules. As a result, if an official is carrying out the rules, or is acting strictly in accordance with them, then, no matter how unjust the results are for the citizen, no question of maladministration can arise. This appears to be the point of view adopted in the report of 1961 by JUSTICE, *The Citizen and the Administration: the redress of grievances,*

[19] Para. 322.

[20] This is extracted from the First Annual Report of the Northern Ireland Commissioner for Complaints, 1970, para. 20. See article by H. J. Elcock (1972) 50 *Public Administration* 87–93.

where it is stated that "complaints against administrative acts merely because they give effect to laws which are considered objectionable or in some way undesirable . . . are not in fact complaints against bad administration but against bad laws."[21] I cannot agree with this point of view. Such complaints are, in many cases, complaints both against bad administration and bad laws, and it is the bad laws which have made possible and sometimes made obligatory the bad administration. If we can say: "Hard cases make bad law" we can say also: "Bad law makes hard cases"!

While it may be asserted that acts of officials which are contrary to law are clearly examples of maladministration, it does not follow that acts of officials which are in accordance with law cannot be examples of maladministration. The cause of maladministration sometimes is that it is the result of a "bad" law or rule, bad because it is ambiguous, obscure, self-contradictory, obstructive, or bad because it embodies in itself principles of discrimination, bias, injustice which inevitably produce maladministration. If the law is an Act of Parliament, the official may have no alternative but to produce maladministration, although he may attempt, or a court of law may attempt, by interpretation of the Act, to avoid or evade or reduce the unjust consequences of the Act, so far as lies in their power. The remedy for maladministration of this kind may not be directed towards the official, but may have to reach back to Parliament. On the other hand if the law is embodied in a rule made by officials under powers delegated by Parliament or as a departmental rule governing the conduct of business, then the remedy may lie against the officials or the depart-

[21] Called sometimes the Whyatt Report after its chairman Sir John Whyatt, para. 71.

ment who made the law. The main point is, however, that a bad law may cause maladministration and that although the remedy against such maladministration may be different from that to be employed when maladministration occurs under what we may for the moment call a " good " law, we must not exclude from our consideration maladministration that arises in this way. And it is for reasons of this kind that I believe that we must adopt the wider meaning of administration and consequently of maladministration, and not mark it off sharply and unrealistically from the process of rule-making, whether by Parliament or by officials.

This is a question that will recur from time to time as we proceed. In the meantime we must admire the wisdom of those who drafted the New Zealand Parliamentary Commissioner (Ombudsman) Act which was passed in 1962, in which no reference was made to administration or maladministration thus avoiding frustrating arguments about definitions, while at the same time the possibility of a " bad " law was recognised explicitly. The Ombudsman in New Zealand is empowered to report upon any decision, recommendation, act or omission which, in his opinion,

(a) appears to have been contrary to law;
(b) was unreasonable, unjust, oppressive, or improperly discriminatory, or was in accordance with *a rule of law or a provision of any enactment or a practice* that is or may be unreasonable, unjust, oppressive or improperly discriminatory; or
(c) was based wholly or partly on a mistake of law or fact; or
(d) was wrong.[22]

22 New Zealand Statutes 1962, No. 10, s. 19. My italics.

Can it all be summed up in those resounding simple words at the end—" was wrong " !

III

It is not advisable, in this short space, to attempt a general analysis of the causes of maladministration. As our exposition proceeds, however, it is inevitable that the discussion of remedies may involve, if only intermittently, some passing reference to causes. But there are two or three things which are worth saying at this stage.

The first is that some examples of maladministration or of types of maladministration arise out of the pursuit of objects which would generally be regarded as good. Thus the attempt to treat citizens with justice and equity can lead to a multiplication of rules and precedents which officials must apply or create so that each citizen gets what he is entitled to, and that he is not more or less favourably treated than another citizen similarly situated. This produces form filling or file keeping on a grand scale. It produces also a meticulous, careful, cautious, correct attitude to the consideration of citizens' claims, and this in turn produces delay. A large part of the administration of the social services in Britain is concerned with questions of this kind, in which it is of the greatest importance that justice should be done to and between claimants for these services. Or again, in the process of safeguarding the public purse, of ensuring that the taxpayers' money should be rightly spent, not wasted or misused—in itself not a contemptible object—most complicated procedures and routines may be devised to ensure orderliness and regularity in the public accounts and responsibility and control in the authorising of expenditure. All this will produce delay. Yet this delay may, in its turn, produce hardship or injustice for the citizen. It leads some people to say, from time to time, that, as a general rule, what we want is not the right answer so much as a quick answer. More often than not, it is alleged, the quick answer will produce justice by its very speed. But, while it is easy to say, in relation to public administration by officials, that there must be no " undue " delay, what is " undue " delay is not so easy to say. Fairness and speed do not inevitably go together.

The second point is that some examples of maladministration arise from things that are bad. If the level of ability of government officials is lower than it should be for the tasks they are to perform, errors in administration will occur. The quality of the staff which departments can recruit is of considerable importance. This was the kind of problem which the Fulton Committee had to consider in making its recommendations for an improved and more efficient civil service. In the course of their inquiry, also, they found themselves led to the conclusion that a barrier to better administration was unnecessary secrecy in the governmental process and they recommended that the government should set up an inquiry to make recommendations for getting rid of unnecessary secrecy.[23] Here again there is great difficulty in saying what is and what is not unnecessary secrecy. This topic has been thoroughly examined by a committee of inquiry under the chairmanship of Lord Franks which reported in 1972.[24] And it is interesting that in a report by JUSTICE entitled *Administration under Law*, pub-

[23] Cmnd. 3638, paras. 277–280.
[24] Cmnd. 5104.

lished in 1971,[25] a principal recommendation was that certain principles of good administration should be laid down and enforced upon officials and within these principles great stress was placed upon the importance of giving to citizens full and accurate information of what is proposed before decisions are taken, so that representations may be made in advance. A lack of information, at the right time and in the right quantity for citizens affected by official action was, in the opinion of this report, an important cause of maladministration.

The third point is that while maladministration may arise from things that we may think of as good or from things that we may think of as bad, it arises also from conditions which are, in a large measure, unavoidable, inescapable, and nobody's fault. The sheer complication and difficulty of some subjects with which officials must deal in applying the law accounts for some measure of maladministration. Taxation is a notorious example. The whole subject is for most citizens almost completely unintelligible. The form he has to fill in has been greatly simplified but the notes he has to read baffle almost every taxpayer. It is difficult to see how the basic difficulty of the subject can be somehow conjured away. For officials as for citizens the technicality is so great that only a few experts can be expected to understand it. It is not surprising that officials make mistakes in this area. It is not necessary to have recourse to theories of conspiracy against the citizens' purse or of intentional obscurity in the publications of the Department of Inland Revenue to explain why that Department heads the league table for complaints of maladministra-

[25] Stevens & Son.

tion from taxpayers.[26] In the administration of social services, similarly, there is a great measure of unavoidable complication in the rules and decisions covering unemployment insurance, entitlement to payments, supplementary benefits and so on which is extremely difficult for the average official to understand, much less explain to the citizen. A Member of Parliament expressed the position vividly when he said: ". . . a number of people are absolutely overwhelmed by bureaucracy, and, quite frankly, after ten minutes with some of our officials at the Ministry they are lucky if they know what day it is . . . they are absolutely bamboozled by the procedures which are terribly well known to the Ministry but not to the general public." [27] He does not exaggerate the state of mind of the citizens in many of these areas; he may indeed exaggerate the grasp which officials themselves can be expected to acquire as they struggle with new waves of regulations.

In the pages that follow I shall discuss the operation and effectiveness of certain selected institutions in Britain through which remedies against maladministration by government officials may be sought. I should confess at the outset that, as a member of the Franks Committee on Tribunals and Inquiries, which reported in 1957,[28] my approach to this subject is still very much on the lines adopted in that Report. To this extent I have learnt nothing. If an apology is called for, I give it now, once and for all. And in particular, I lead into the next stage of my exposition in the way in which the Franks Report opened up the discussion of its own subject-matter.

26 H.C. 334 of 1971–72, p. 36, Qu. 223.
27 Mr. Dan Jones in H.C. 334 of 1971–72, p. 32, Qu. 204.
28 Cmnd. 218.

Decisions are made by administrative bodies in the process of applying the law and from time to time citizens object to these decisions. When they do so, a further decision becomes necessary. "This further decision is of a different kind: whether to confirm, cancel or vary the original decision. In reaching it account must be taken not only of the original decision, but also of the objection."[29] In Britain there are a number of ways in which a further decision may be sought. There may be resort to a court; there may be resort to a tribunal specially constituted to deal with these disputes; there may be an appeal to a Minister, that is to a central government department, with provision for a statutory inquiry at some stage into the issues or some part of them involved in the dispute; there may be recourse to a Member of Parliament with a request that he take the matter up with the department or raise the matter in the House by question or motion or otherwise; there may be a protest in the newspapers or through a professional or trade organisation or through an advisory or consultative body attached to a department; or there may be action through local councillors or by a visit to local government offices, and so on. In these and other ways, citizens who believe that they have been wrongly treated or have suffered some act of maladministration, may pursue the matter with a view to getting the decision explained, justified, modified or cancelled. That these ways of obtaining redress vary in effectiveness is admitted and will be illustrated as we proceed.

We begin with those arrangements by which the redress of grievances are dealt with through courts, tribunals and

[29] *Ibid.*, paras. 7 and 8.

certain kinds of inquiries out of which a further decision comes. Whether this kind of provision is appropriate to the cases submitted to it or adequate in dealing with them is open to discussion. Whether it should be extended is an important question. But first of all it is necessary to see how courts and tribunals work, and thereafter to consider how effective they are in providing remedies for maladministration.

CHAPTER 2

COURTS

I

BEFORE we consider the function of the courts in remedying maladministration, it is advisable to say something about the nature and functions of tribunals and inquiries.[1] At the outset of its Report the Franks Committee made three important points about them. The first was that the object of Parliament in making special provision for tribunals and inquiries, and in keeping these decisions away from the ordinary courts and from the ordinary course of administration, was " to promote good administration." Administration must not only be efficient in the sense that the objectives of policy are securely attained without delay. It must also satisfy the general body of citizens that it is proceeding with reasonable regard to the balance between the public interest which it promotes and the private interest which it disturbs. Parliament has, we infer, intended that the further decisions, or, as they may rightly be termed in this context, adjudications must be acceptable as having been properly made.[2] There was here the idea that if these decisions were reached by a process which citizens did not regard as proper it would amount to maladministration.

[1] I must acknowledge my great debt, in my attempt to expound the themes of this chapter, to the masterly survey of the whole subject by Bernard Schwartz and H. W. R. Wade entitled *Legal Control of Government* (Oxford, Clarendon Press, 1972).

[2] Cmnd. 218, paras. 20 and 21.

The second feature of the analysis in the Franks Report was to say openly that " tribunals are not ordinary courts, but neither are they appendages of government departments. . . . We consider that tribunals should properly be regarded as machinery provided by Parliament for adjudication rather than as part of the machinery of administration." [3]

And finally the Committee deliberately turned its back on pursuing the analysis of such concepts as judicial, quasi-judicial, administrative, the rule of law and so on as a guide to the control of, or the allocation of powers to, tribunals, the ordinary courts, or to statutory inquiries. Instead it adopted the proposition " that there are certain general and closely linked characteristics which should mark their special procedures. We call these characteristics openness, fairness and impartiality. Take openness. If the procedures were wholly secret, the basis of confidence and acceptability would be lacking. Next take fairness. If the objector were not allowed to state his case, there would be nothing to stop oppression. Thirdly, there is impartiality. How can the citizen be satisfied unless he feels that those who decide his case come to their decision with open minds? " [4]

These statements were considered at the time to be a little low-brow, almost banal, by some academic students of the subject. But, in my opinion, they were a valuable guide to deciding how tribunals and inquiries should be organised so as to ensure good administration. They state conditions, too, the absence of which in the conduct of government, indicate the marks of maladministration.

[3] Para. 40.
[4] Paras. 23 and 24.

II

It is unnecessary to follow the detailed study of tribunals carried out by the Franks Committee. The point of interest is to see what has been done to ensure that the tribunals are so organised that they ensure that the objections of a citizen to the decisions of authority are properly considered and that the " further decision," as it was called, is properly made. In line with their objects of openness, fairness and impartiality, they recommended that, as a general rule, hearings should be in public; the right to legal representation before tribunals should be curtailed only in the most exceptional circumstances; every care should be taken to ensure that the citizen is aware of and fully understands his right to apply to a tribunal and should know, in good time before the hearing, the case which he will have to meet; parties should be free to question witnesses directly and not only through the chairman; decisions should be reasoned and as full as possible; chairmen of tribunals exercising appellate functions should have legal qualifications and so, ordinarily, should chairmen of tribunals of first instance; there should be an appeal on fact, law and merits from a tribunal of first instance to an appellate tribunal except where the tribunal of first instance is exceptionally strong and well qualified; and no statute should contain words purporting to oust the supervisory jurisdiction of the courts by way of the remedies of certiorari, prohibition and mandamus.

These and other reforms were embodied in the Tribunals and Inquiries Act of 1958 [5] which set up, as recommended by the Franks Committee, a Council on Tribunals to super-

[5] Now replaced by a consolidating statute, the Tribunals and Inquiries Act 1971.

vise the operation of tribunals. The reports of this Council give a good idea of the extent to which tribunals are used in Britain and the kind of problems which arise in their operation. The object of the reforms and of the functions given to the Council on Tribunals is to ensure both that the law is administered effectively and that citizens can feel at the same time that they have had fair and just treatment. Tribunals must be seen to be independent of the government. Their chairmen and members are not government officials. Their powers are derived from Act of Parliament. It is true that their clerks are usually civil servants, belonging to the Ministry concerned, and to this extent there is a possibility of influence being exerted on members by the department. The remedy here must lie in appointing a strong chairman. This is a matter to which the Council on Tribunals has given attention.[6] It is important, too, that there should be an appeal on a point of law from the decisions of tribunals save in the most exceptional circumstances. In addition to this there is recourse to the High Court for a review of a decision. ". . . the position has been transformed by the revival of judicial review for error on the face of the record."[7] Thus, in the case of certain tribunals from which there is no appeal to the courts on law—the National Insurance Tribunals from whom appeal goes to Commissioners, the Supplementary Benefit Appeal Tribunals, the National Health Service Tribunal, and the Betting Levy Appeal Tribunals—there is, nevertheless recourse to the courts for review of the record and these tribunals, therefore, do not fall outside the ordinary system of the law.

6 Schwartz and Wade, *op cit.*, p. 162.
7 *Ibid.*, p. 158.

Whenever new procedural regulations are made or old regulations are altered, the Council on Tribunals must be consulted, and it makes it its business to see that each set of rules conforms to the best practice and discusses many points of detail with the departments.[8] It tries to simplify and consolidate rules where possible, or it encourages the production of explanatory booklets and leaflets to help people to understand their rights.[9] It has approved of the idea that the use of the legal rules of evidence is probably a doubtful blessing in many of these informal proceedings.[10] It has encouraged the making of procedural rules by which tribunals are required to give reasons for their decisions. The Act of 1958 gave a broad dispensing power to the Lord Chancellor to direct that any class of decisions should be exempted from the necessity to give reasons, subject to his first consulting the Council on Tribunals. He did this in 1959 but, on the advice of the Council, he refused the requests.[11]

The position is summed up by Schwartz and Wade in *Legal Control of Government* as follows: ". . . it may be said that the work of tribunals has been improved by the Act of 1958 and the continuing efforts which date from that statute. Tribunals are now seen to be an integral part of the machinery of justice, related directly to the courts through the channels of appeal and judicial review, and aiming at the best practicable level of fairness in procedure. With something like 2,000 separate tribunals in operation, it cannot be expected that all will work equally well or that there will be no complaints."[12]

8 p. 153.
9 p. 154.
10 p. 155. See Annual Report of Council of Tribunals for 1966, para. 63.
11 p. 156. Annual Report for 1959, paras. 58–69.
12 p. 162.

III

Although tribunals and inquiries are often bracketed together in the course of discussion, they are different in purpose and function. It is worth recalling some words from the Report of the Franks Committee when they were discussing the application of their criteria of openness, fairness and impartiality. ". . . The method by which a Minister arrives at a decision after a hearing or inquiry cannot be the same as that by which a tribunal arrives at a decision . . . When Parliament sets up a tribunal to decide cases, the adjudication is placed outside the Department concerned. The members of the tribunal are neutral and impartial in relation to the policy of the Minister, except in so far as that policy is contained in the rules which the tribunal is set up to apply. But the Minister, in deciding cases, is committed to a policy which he has been charged by Parliament to carry out. In this sense he is not, and cannot be, impartial."[13] As Schwartz and Wade put it: "So far from being a recognised part of the machinery of legal justice, as tribunals are, inquiries are concerned with acts of policy for which a Minister is responsible to Parliament. The object is to assist the Minister to arrive at the best decision in the public interest, not to establish individual rights."[14]

But as they go on to say, "the demand for administrative justice is almost as strong as the demand for legal justice, and public opinion is very sensitive about procedural fairness." And it was here that the Franks Committee made certain proposals for reform. Objectors had had no right to know the reasons for the proposals they were objecting to. The Franks Committee recommended that an agency or

[13] Para. 25.

[14] *Op. cit.*, p. 163.

planning authority should be required to make available, in good time before the inquiry, a written statement giving full particulars of its case, and the deciding Minister should, whenever possible, make available before the inquiry a statement of the policy relevant to the particular case.[15] Next, the report of the inspector who held the inquiry and advised the Minister was (as a rule) not published. The Franks Committee recommended that the complete text of the report should accompany the Minister's letter of decision and also be available on request centrally and locally.[16] Thirdly, a Minister normally gave no reasons for his decision, and here the recommendation was "that the Minister's letter of decision should set out in full his findings and inferences of fact and the reasons for the decision." [17] These recommendations were accepted by the government and brought into effect either by statute or by a change in administrative procedure.

And from the adoption of these changes and of the rules of procedure laid down concerning inquiries, new scope was created for judicial review. "It can now be seen whether the minister was acting on wrong legal grounds or irrelevant considerations, and it is now common for decisions to be questioned for such reasons." Furthermore the court is prepared to quash merely because the reasons are unsatisfactory, since there is then a breach of the statutory duty to give reasons. This was done, for instance, where the reasons given were so obscure that there was real doubt as to what they really were." [18]

[15] Paras. 281, 287–288.
[16] Para. 344.
[17] Para. 352.
[18] Schwartz and Wade, *op. cit.*, p. 167. Statutory requirement is in the Act of 1958, s. 12 (1). The case referred to is *Givaudan & Co. Ltd.* v. *Minister of Housing and Local Government* [1967] 1 W.L.R. 250.

It is interesting to notice that the inspectors who conduct the inquiries are, in England, as a rule officials of the Ministry. The Franks Committee had recommended that they should be placed under the control of the Lord Chancellor, so that they should be publicly seen to be independent,[19] but this was not done. This situation is generally accepted, though it is significant that in Scotland the inspector is generally an independent person. Schwartz and Wade express this opinion: " It is essential for inspectors to be in close touch with the policies of their departments, otherwise there will be an excessive number of wrong decisions; and it may be positively misleading to encourage people to suppose that the inspector's function is to make an objective assessment like that of a judge, when in reality he must weigh the facts of each case in the balance of policy and recommend what is politic rather than what is required by law." [20] In any case since rules of procedure for the conduct of an inquiry are now laid down, and the inspector's reports are published, and the Minister must give reasons for his decision, there are valuable safeguards to ensure openness and fairness which, in this sort of process, is what the citizen is entitled to claim. The chief complaint the citizen can make now is that of delay, for which the procedure for inquiry and all its safeguards must take some share of the blame.[21]

In its oversight of public inquiries as also of tribunals the Council on Tribunals is an important body. Its terms of reference include the power to consider and report on such matters as it may consider to be of special importance with

[19] Report, para. 303.

[20] *Op. cit.*, p. 171.

[21] The authoritative work on the subject of inquiries is R. E. Wraith and G. B. Lamb, *Public Inquiries as an Instrument of Government* (Allen & Unwin, 1971).

respect to administrative procedures involving or which may involve the holding by or on behalf of a Minister of a statutory inquiry or any such procedure. A judgment upon the effectiveness of the Council is not easy to make from the outside. It will be noticed, when we come later on to deal with the work of the British Ombudsman (who is *ex officio* a member of the Council), that he himself undertakes the investigation of complaints about the conduct of inquiries and the subsequent taking of decisions by Ministries in relation to them. This suggests that a task which the Council might be expected to undertake has, for some reason, gone elsewhere. It seems clear also that the Ombudsman is well equipped to deal with these complaints effectively.

We are able, however, to get at least one authoritative inside opinion about the Council's work. Professor H. W. R. Wade was a member of it from its institution until 1971. He remarks that " its membership is not ideally suited to its work." [22] By this he means that it needs more lawyers! As a layman I must confess that I think it odd, in view of the nature of the Council's work, that its secretary is not a lawyer and preferably, I should think, its chairman also. In the second place, the Council is, in Professor Wade's opinion, ineffective. It needs to be geared, somehow, to the parliamentary machine.[23] He quotes an extract from the annual report of the Council for 1969–70 where it says " that departments should consult us on proposals concerning tribunals at the earliest possible stage, before decisions have become virtually irrevocable. Final decisions ought not to be taken on matters on which we are at issue with a department until we have had an opportunity of putting our case

[22] In Schwartz and Wade, *op. cit.*, pp. 179–180.
[23] *Ibid.*, p. 180.

fully to the Lord Chancellor. In addition we think that there ought probably to be some machinery for making our views publicly known when Bills are before Parliament, since otherwise important provisions about tribunals may be enacted without any knowledge that we have studied them and made recommendations. One possible arrangement might be on the lines of section 108 of the National Insurance Act 1965, under which the reports of the National Insurance Advisory Committee have to be laid before Parliament along with the regulations to which they refer."[24]

On the other hand, a permanent body now exists with the task of considering the problems of tribunals and inquiries. It has produced distinct results. Its main task, in Professor Wade's opinion, is "to secure that all the various tribunals and inquiries are treated as a *system*, with common principles of procedure and a coherent overall pattern."[25]

IV

Perhaps the most important part of the oversight of tribunals and inquiries, however, is directed to ensure that they act in accordance with the law. This applies also, of course, to the whole range of administrative action. The most obvious of all forms of maladministration is illegal action. And in this area it is to the ordinary courts of law that we must look for remedies. How extensive are they?

To begin with, the state may be sued in ordinary civil actions of tort or contract just as if it were an ordinary litigant. This has been established on a statutory basis by the Crown Proceedings Act of 1947. Although the Act did

[24] Para. 48.
[25] p. 180.

not alter the fundamental rule of personal liability of servants of the Crown, most plaintiffs naturally prefer to sue the Crown rather than the individual. Crown privilege—the government's power to prevent evidence being given in court where it is claimed that its disclosure would be against the public interest—was not dealt with by the Crown Proceedings Act and it remained as a barrier against the citizen obtaining a remedy in certain cases. A decision of the House of Lords in 1968 [26] overruled its earlier decision of 1942 [27] in which the House had laid down that an affidavit of the Minister was conclusive. They made it clear in 1968 that, though the courts would naturally respect claims based on genuine secrets of state, they would not allow other claims unless the public interest in secrecy outweighs the public interest in doing justice to the litigant, and—here is the essential point—this is to be determined by the court and not by the executive.

The wider powers of the British courts to control action by officials are based upon the doctrine of *ultra vires* and, in a more restricted area, on error on the face of the record. So far as *ultra vires* is concerned the principle is: "If an act is within the powers granted, it is valid. If it is outside them, it is void." Somehow cases have to be brought within this principle. If necessary "the court reads the statute as containing an implied limitation that the administrative decision shall be reasonable or that it shall conform to certain implied purposes or that particular facts shall exist. It is assumed that Parliament cannot have intended otherwise." [28] With "error on the face of the record," the decision is ad-

[26] *Conway* v. *Rimmer* [1968] A.C. 910.
[27] *Duncan* v. *Cammell Laird & Co. Ltd.* [1942] A.C. 624.
[28] Schwartz and Wade, *op. cit.*, p. 210.

mitted to be *intra vires*, but is, for example, a reasoned decision based upon some misinterpretation of the law.

The simple situation in which the citizen would look to the courts for assistance against acts of maladministration would be, first, a failure by the official to take some action which it was his duty to take; secondly, the use of a power for a purpose for which it was not intended; thirdly, the use of a power beyond the limits placed upon it, though not for an unauthorised purpose. There are well-known remedies in English law for these situations and they may be briefly noticed. There are the remedies of private law: damages, injunctions and declaratory judgments. Beside them are the "prerogative" remedies of certiorari, prohibition, mandamus and habeas corpus. Certiorari calls a public authority to account for exceeding or abusing its power. Mandamus calls for the proper discharge of some public duty, and is available against Ministers of the Crown as well as other public authorities. It plays an important and efficient part in public law.[29]

But the verdict on the remedies is this. "One of the best features of administrative law in Britain is in the range and effectiveness of the remedies. Its worst feature, by general consent, is the thicket of technicality and inconsistency which surrounds them." [30] And the Law Commission, in a submission to the Lord Chancellor in May 1969, referred to "a widely held feeling that the remedies available in the courts for the review and control of administrative action are in urgent need of rationalisation. The procedural complexities and anomalies which face the litigant

[29] *Ibid.*, p. 220.
[30] *Ibid.*, p. 216.

who seeks an order of certiorari, prohibition or mandamus have long been the subject of criticism, while the circumstances in which injunctions and declarations are obtainable would also appear to call for review. The law of judicial control, it has been argued, is at present at the mercy of a formulary system of remedies. The technicalities and uncertainties which, mainly for historical reasons, are a feature of judicial control of public authorities under our legal system contrast sharply with the simplicity with which administrative proceedings may be started in other systems *e.g.* that of France." [31] The Law Commission urged the Lord Chancellor to set up a Royal Commission to inquire into this and other questions of administrative law. But the request was refused.

In rejecting the proposal for a Royal Commission, the Lord Chancellor asked the Law Commission to review the existing remedies for the judicial control of administrative acts and omissions with a view to evolving a simpler and more effective procedure. The Law Commission produced in October 1971 a working paper [32] intended for circulation to persons and bodies interested with a view to comment and criticism. In this paper they reiterated their views on the unsatisfactory nature of the remedies available. "The prerogative orders," they wrote, "are bedevilled by a complex and restrictive procedure and practice. It is a weakness of the orders that discovery of documents cannot be obtained. Moreover it may be that a potential applicant who did not know of the illegality of the administrative action for some time after it was taken will be unable to use the

[31] Cmnd. 4059.
[32] The Law Commission: Published Working Paper No. 40, *Remedies in Administrative Law.*

orders after the lapse of six months. Again, it is not clear whether certiorari is only available when there is a duty on the part of the deciding authority 'to act judicially' whatever that may mean. It is for consideration whether the courts should not be more ready to admit oral evidence and permit cross-examination."[33]

While none of these restrictions applies to declaratory relief or injunctions, which were seen at one time as "new and up-to-date machinery" replacing the old pick and shovel methods,[34] it is apparent nevertheless that there are limitations upon the effectiveness of the declaration. ". . . it will not be granted to challenge the decision of a tribunal for error of law on the face of the record, at least where a declaration to that effect would be of no avail to the applicant. Moreover, on the most recent authority the requirement of standing is more strict for declarations (and much more for injunctions according to established authority) than for prerogative orders."[35] The Law Commission sums up its views thus: "The truth is, therefore, that the prerogative orders on the one hand, and the declarations and injunctions on the other, each have advantages and disadvantages compared to the other. Nothing except history justifies these distinctions . . . It is not possible to claim them both in the same proceedings. The litigant may thus be confronted with a difficult choice. The position seems to us to be wholly unreasonable."[36]

The Law Commission put forward therefore, as their provisional view, the proposal that there should be a single

[33] Working Paper No. 40, para. 70.
[34] Lord Denning, *Freedom under the Law* (1949), p. 126.
[35] Working Paper No. 40, para. 71.
[36] *Ibid.*, para. 72.

remedy and procedure for the judicial review of administrative actions and orders, which might be called "the application for review."[37] "Under this single procedure," they wrote, "we envisage that the applicant would be able to ask for any form of relief at present obtainable for the control of administrative action in the High Court. Thus the applicant seeking review might ask the court to *quash* the particular administrative decision or order, to *enjoin* the administrative authority from exceeding its jurisdiction or powers, to *command* the authority to act where it is under a duty to do so, or to *declare* the action or order invalid and of no effect. The court could grant the form of relief requested, or where this was not suitable in the circumstances, any other appropriate relief. In suitable cases the court might also on an application for review declare the legal rights of the applicant."[38] This proposal, though relatively simple to make or state, involves many consequential problems, and in particular questions of *locus standi,* time limits, and exclusion clauses. The working paper deals with them lucidly, putting forward arguments on both sides. It is not necessary to go into detail about them here.[39] One final point in their proposals should be mentioned. To the question: "To which courts will the application for review lie?" the answer they prefer is "that a single judge selected from a panel of those experienced in administrative law should entertain the application for review with power on the application for leave to assign difficult cases to a full Divisional Court." What is significant in their proposal is in the sentence: "The *specialised* supervisory jurisdiction

[37] *Ibid.*, paras. 75 *et seq.*
[38] *Ibid.*, para. 75.
[39] They are summarised in para. 154.

which we regard as essential to the consistent application of principles of administrative law could be secured by the assignment of judges with particular experience of administrative law to hear applications for review." [40]

There the matter rested at the time of writing.

V

Two references in the publications of the Law Commission on the subject of remedies in administrative law stick out significantly. The first, already mentioned, occurs in their submission to the Lord Chancellor in May 1969 and refers to "the simplicity with which administrative proceedings may be started in other systems *e.g.* that of France." The second is found in the working paper discussed above where the Commission refers to the position in the United States where "the petition for review" is an example of a single remedy available for the control of administrative action. It is upon this model that the Commission recommends the adoption of the "application for review" in Britain, preferring "application" to "petition" on the ground that the latter does not assert sufficiently the *right* of the subject to redress.[41] Surely this is the point at which our attention is recalled to Miss Hamlyn's object "that the common people of the United Kingdom may realise the privileges which in law and custom they enjoy in comparison with other European peoples." How does their situation compare with that of other peoples in this matter of judicial remedies and their access to them? We can ask the more precise question: what have the people of

[40] Para. 138, my italics.
[41] Para. 75.

some other countries got which the people of Britain have not got and ought to have? And let us begin with the first part of the question: what have the peoples of some other countries got in the way of judicial remedies?

For a long time it has been customary to point to France as an example of a country whose people are especially blessed in this regard, and especially so in comparison with Britain. I shall try to state the French citizen's position briefly and generally.[42] If a citizen of France has a complaint or objection against the administration, if he requires what the Franks Committee called " a further decision," he is entitled to seek redress, and he seeks it in a set of specialised courts, at the head of which is the *Conseil d'Etat*, endowed with a general competence to review all administrative acts. There is a two-tier system, with the lower consisting of twenty-four *Tribunaux Administratifs* which act as the courts of first instance in the regions, and from whose decisions an appeal may be taken to the *Conseil d'Etat*. In addition there are certain specialised tribunals[43] empowered to take decisions on, for example, public accounts, national service, professional conduct, public assistance, education and so on, and from the decisions of these bodies recourse may be had to the *Conseil d'Etat* not on appeal, but for *cassation*, or as we would say " review," with the object of questioning the decision.

The position may be summarised by saying that the *Conseil d'Etat* receives cases either at first instance (*e.g.* proceedings

[42] I find this difficult to do, because it seems to me that there are so many exceptions to any general statement. My account is based principally on L. N. Brown and J. F. Garner, *French Administrative Law* (London, Butterworth, 1967); and the evidence of Monsieur M. Letourneur, of the *Conseil d'Etat* before the Franks Committee on February 21, 1957 (Minutes of Evidence, 27th day).

[43] There is a list of them in Brown and Garner, *op. cit.*, Appendix A.

to annul a decree of the government would be taken straight to the *Conseil*); or on appeal on law or on merits from the decisions of the regional *Tribunaux Administratifs*; or on review (*cassation*) from a specialised tribunal, which the French describe as administrative " jurisdictions." [44] Stating the position from the point of view of the citizen, he can take his complaint to the regional tribunal and, if he wishes, on appeal to the *Conseil d'Etat*, or, if his complaint has gone to an " administrative jurisdiction," he can seek a review of the decision by *cassation* before the *Conseil d'Etat*. We are told that the procedure is simple and cheap. " The proceedings are informal," said M. Letourneur to the Franks Committee, " and the *recours* does not have to be well written. But if the plaintiff wishes to have help he can get it from the town hall, for instance, or from anybody." [45] The simplicity of the remedies themselves is also stressed by writers on the French system. " Charged as they are with a general competence to review all administrative acts, the French administrative courts," write Brown and Garner, " have utilised for this purpose three, and only three, simple forms of action, namely, the *recours pour exces de pouvoir* and the *recours en cassation* in matters of legality, and the *recours de pleine juridiction* where damages or public relief are sought. Between them the three remedies cover all the ground, save only the tiny enclave within which *actes du gouvernement* have now been fenced." [46] We are told also that " the plaintiff before the administrative courts is not in practice required to choose his ground of complaint. . . ." [47] We are bound to recall here not only the number but also the

[44] Brown and Garner, *op. cit.*, pp. 23–27.
[45] Evidence, Qu. 6118.
[46] p. 133.
[47] p. 127.

complexities surrounding the remedies available in Britain, to which the Law Commission made a reference.

To the advantages of simplicity of procedure and cheapness, there is added for the French citizen the merit that his case is decided by people who are expert in administrative matters and apply a specialised branch of the law which has been developed to protect the citizen, the *administré*, as the French call him, from the administration. It is stressed [48] that the administrative courts do not merely annul administrative acts, from those of Minister to mayor, on the ground that they are *ultra vires*. They also protect the citizen from the use of administrative powers that, even when within the bounds of technical legality, have, in the judgment of the *Conseil*, been used for purposes which the legislator did not intend. This check on the misuse of powers (*détournement de pouvoir*) is, indeed, one of the most effective of the *Conseil's* methods of protecting individuals from executive encroachments and bureaucratic rule. At the same time it is claimed to be an advantage that the *Conseil d'Etat* is a body composed predominantly of administrators; its functions include advising the government on administrative matters, advising it on the meaning of laws and regulations. Indeed four of the five sections into which the *Conseil* is divided are concerned with its administrative functions and only one (the *section du contentieux*) with its judicial or adjudicatory functions, but it is this last section which is most powerful.[49]

48 By Dorothy Pickles in *The Government and Politics of France*, Vol. 1, p. 295 (Methuen, 1972).

49 It is interesting to notice that its members do not enjoy the same security of tenure in law as the judges of the ordinary courts, headed by the *Cour de Cassation*, but in practice there is no difference. Brown and Garner, *op. cit.*, p. 39.

So far as one can judge from what is written about the system of *droit administratif* in France, it would seem that the French citizen has available to him some things which the British citizen has not got and should have. The first is a process of seeking remedies which is cheap. How far cheapness extends is not entirely clear. Lawyers are employed in certain proceedings before the *Conseil d'Etat*. But over a wide area of the ordinary citizen's concern, the process is cheap. The work is done, in fact, by the officials of the administrative courts themselves, both regional and central. A second advantage is the simplicity of the remedies themselves in comparison with the complexity and uncertainty of those available in Britain. This is accepted in Britain and, as we have seen, proposals have been made to improve the position. And a third point is that, in the words of Professor H. W. R. Wade, " the most obvious advantage of the French system is that it is much more specialised so that both the judges and their *commissaires*, as well as the advocates, are highly skilled administrative lawyers. The subject therefore has much more solidity and consistency than in Britain." [50] But has this advantage no attendant disadvantage? Does it matter that the *droit administratif* is cut off from the mainstream of the law? We must look at this point a little more closely.

Consider first a disadvantage that arises in France itself —the question of conflict of jurisdictions. If disputes against the administration are to be taken to a specialised set of courts and other cases to be taken to the " ordinary " courts, who is to decide and, more important, upon what principles is it to be decided, where the boundary line falls? The

[50] In Schwartz and Wade, *Legal Control of Government*, pp. 323–24.

question of who is to decide presents no difficulty—since 1872 there has been established the *Tribunal des Conflits*, composed of an equal number of judges (five) from the *Conseil d'Etat* and from the *Cour de Cassation*, the two supreme bodies in the respective jurisdictions. We are told that the number of cases arising before the *Tribunal* is not large. On the other hand all authorities seem to agree that the rules which determine the dividing line between the two jurisdictions are extremely complex, and, in the opinion of one French expert, of "excessive technicality."[51] It is proper, therefore, to admit that this is a defect in the French system. It is a price paid for the advantages of a specialised *droit administratif*. Whether the price need be so high is another question; there is no obvious necessity about it. But no doubt the reform of such a subject, containing as it does some of the subtlest distinctions in French law, is extremely difficult, if not impossible—more difficult probably than the reform of the technicalities of the British remedies to which the Law Commission has been giving its attention. In the meantime it is necessary to record that there is a price to pay. The French lawyer is presented "with a critical problem at the very threshold of his task of obtaining redress for his client, namely, to which of the two sets of courts must the case in hand be brought?"[52] And there may be occasions when a French citizen, having brought his case before the wrong jurisdiction, and having only the satisfaction of knowing that all he has achieved is one more

[51] Professor Weil, "The Strength and Weakness of French Administrative Law" [1965] C.L.J. at p. 252, quoted in Brown and Garner, *op. cit.*, p. 136.

[52] Brown and Garner, *op. cit.*, p. 58. The whole topic is lucidly explained in Chapter 6.

decision in the large body of case-law on conflicts of jurisdiction, may be inclined to exclaim as a distinguished British judge has done (extra-judicially) that the remedy in France is worse than the disease.[53]

Delay in the decision of cases is an admitted defect of the French system. I think that, in an odd way, this is connected with one reason for the cheapness of the French procedure, namely, the fact that the case is dealt with by the officials of the *Tribunal Administratif* and the *Conseil d'Etat* themselves, without, as a rule, legal representation. The French procedure is inquisitorial rather than adversarial (as in Britain or the United States), and once the case goes into the machine, it is lost to sight until an answer emerges. When one reads the account of the procedure followed, as set out in the textbooks,[54] one is impressed with the care taken to see that all sides of the case are examined, but at the same time one is impressed with the air of leisureliness and academic detachment with which it is all conducted. It is estimated that, at present, a case in the *Tribunaux Administratifs* takes on an average about eighteen months to be decided, and in the *Conseil d'Etat*, from lodging the case in the registry up to judgment, the average time is also eighteen months. This is a long time to wait for justice. It is true that the position was worse still before the regional tribunals were established as a result of reforms in 1953. It is true, also, we are told, that these times compare not unfavourably with the time taken in the ordinary civil courts. There is not much consolation in this reflection. Delay seems to me to be a serious defect of the French system of *droit*

[53] Lord Diplock, "Judicial Control of the Administrative Process" (1971) 24 C.L.P. 1.

[54] *e.g.* Brown and Garner, *op. cit.*, Chapter 5.

administratif; it cannot be explained away. But at the same time it does not (unlike the conflict of jurisdictions) follow necessarily from the nature of the system of specialised courts and simple remedies which are characteristic of the French system.

There is a final defect in the working of the French *droit administratif* which needs a brief mention. There is, in theory at any rate, no means of enforcing a decision of the administrative courts upon the administration itself if it refuses to accept it. Just as the Queen's Bench Division in England cannot issue a prerogative order against the Crown, so the *Conseil d'Etat* cannot order the enforcement of a judgment upon the administration.[55] It is difficult to judge how important this defect of power is in practice. In 1963 an attempt was made, in the course of some considerable reforms, to ensure that the judgments of the *Conseil d'Etat* could be more effectively executed but it is still not clear what the result will be.[56] It is interesting to compare the position of the administrative courts in France with that of the Ombudsman in Britain, for the latter similarly can only advise the administration and hope that they will take the advice. In France, at any rate, there seems little evidence that the attitude of the administration to the *Conseil d'Etat* has produced a feeling among citizens that they will not get justice when the *Conseil d'Etat* has decided in their favour.[57]

[55] The English exception is a small one; the *Conseil d'Etat* is unable to enforce its judgments against the administration over the whole range of its proceedings.

[56] Drago, "Some recent reforms of the French *Conseil d'Etat*" (1964) 3 I.C.L.Q. 1282.

[57] Brown and Garner, *op. cit.*, pp. 54–54.

VI

France is the famous example, in British eyes, of a country where remedies for maladministration are sought through a system of separate and specialised administrative courts, which deal, to adopt the words used by the *Conseil d'Etat* in a famous judgment, with "all litigation between public authorities and third parties, or between public authorities themselves, concerning the execution, non-execution or bad execution of public services."[58] But although it is the famous example and probably the most influential example, it is not the only example. Switzerland, West Germany (both in the federal government and the *länder*), and to a less extent Belgium, have a strong control over their administrators through special administrative courts; in Italy the *Consiglio di Stato* is regarded as rather a pale reflection of the French *Conseil d'Etat*; in Holland there is the *Raad van Staate,* but wide areas of central administrative activity are excluded from its control and, even where it has jurisdiction, its powers of inquisition are inadequate.[59]

The four countries of Scandinavia provide an interesting contrast among themselves. While in Norway and Denmark the ordinary courts exercise review over administrative activity and may declare an administrative act invalid, or quash it or order the authority to withdraw it or modify it and so on, in Sweden and Finland the administration is, to

[58] The case of Terrier, February 6, 1903. Quoted in Brian Chapman, *The Profession of Government* (Allen & Unwin, 1959), p. 186, a book upon which I rely for the opinions expressed in this paragraph.

[59] Chapman, *op. cit.*, p. 212. He deals with the various European countries in Chapters 10 and 11. It seems to me that he under-estimates the strength of the Belgian *Conseil d'Etat*, in relation to the *Raad van Staate* in Holland.

a very large extent, immune from control by the ordinary courts and is subject to administrative courts. In this respect Sweden, and Finland even more so, resemble France. Professor Herlitz in his fascinating book *Elements of Nordic Public Law* [60] says: "Administrative courts are corner-stones of the systems of legal protection in Finland and Sweden like general courts in other countries." [61] And his description of the way in which the Swedish Supreme Administrative Court works recalls the praise given by many writers to the French *droit administratif.* The procedure is uncomplicated, easy, cheap and reliable.[62] The case is conducted in writing; the appellant cannot appear in person. A perfect legal argument is not required; on the other hand the court is expected to be active in the interests of the parties.[63]

In contrast with so much that is found in Europe, control over the administrators in the United States, both in the federal government and in the states, is in the hands of the ordinary courts and exercised by judges of general rather than specialist jurisdictions. But when that general statement has been made, it is necessary to add of this, as of almost everything else in the United States, that the further you go into the subject, the more exceptions you find in the individual states. For the moment what we are interested in is the comparison with the British system, which shares with the United States the same basic position that it is the ordinary courts not specialised courts which exercise the control. But in making comparisons we shall have to distinguish at times the federal government from the states.

[60] P. A. Norstedt, Stockholm, 1969. See esp. pp. 221–236.
[61] p. 231.
[62] p. 234.
[63] p. 232.

A first difference between Britain and the federal government of the United States has been mentioned already in the position of the prerogative orders as a remedy against maladministration. The United States inherited these writs from Britain, but whereas they still survive in Britain, although much criticised, they have been almost entirely abandoned in the *federal* sphere in the United States. The injunction has taken the place of certiorari as the common non-statutory remedy, and with it is combined commonly an action for a declaration that the challenged administrative decision is illegal.[64] But although one or two individual states have made similar reforms—New York State and Illinois are conspicuous examples [65]—most states still retain a system of remedies based upon the prerogative writs. This is, of course, an enormous exception involving remedies over a wide field of administrative actions affecting all the citizens of almost all the individual states of the Union. We must not exaggerate the extent of the reforms in the United States, while acknowledging that in the federal sphere and in states such as New York and Illinois, the American citizen has a simpler remedy than the British citizen.

In another sphere, however, the citizen in Britain is better placed than the citizen of the United States—and surprisingly so—in the sphere of sovereign immunity, by which a government may claim that it cannot be sued without its own consent. It is, of course, extraordinary that in a country where there is no king, where sovereign power is understood to be in the hands of the people, the doctrine should have been accepted that the state was not liable for

64 Schwartz and Wade, *op. cit.*, pp. 221–222.
65 *Ibid.*, pp. 222–225. Illinois uses the " petition for review."

damages inflicted by its agents on private individuals. But the people are sometimes more dictatorial than kings. However, both in the federal sphere in the United States and in Britain at about the same time, an attempt was made to abolish or restrict the doctrine of sovereign immunity by the passing by Congress of the Federal Tort Claims Act in 1946 and by the British Parliament of the Crown Proceedings Act of 1947. The central provision of both Acts is substantially the same, yet it appears that the American Act renders itself much less effective because of the exceptions which it contains.[66] In particular, so far as federal officials are concerned "the central principle today is that officers are immune from liability for torts resulting from the exercise of discretionary functions."[67] This is an extraordinary exception, not found in English or French law. In the individual states, however, where until 1961 it could be stated that the courts of the states had not repudiated the doctrine of sovereign immunity, changes have come about since the decision, in particular, of a Californian case.[68] It is now claimed that "the courts of almost half the states have disallowed, in whole or part, the doctrine of governmental immunity for torts."[69] And it is to be noted that this reform is the work of the ordinary courts, not of legislatures and not of special administrative courts.

From the point of view of the French system and to a large extent also even from the British point of view, what strikes one about the American system of control over the administration, federal and state, is that generally speak-

[66] *Ibid.*, pp. 1194–1197.
[67] *Ibid.*, p. 196.
[68] *Muskopf* v. *Corning Hospital District*, 359 P. 2d 457 (Cal.) 1961.
[69] Schwartz and Wade, *op. cit.*, p. 198.

ing it is over-judicialised. The courts tend to retry administrative proceedings, rather than, as in Britain, to concern themselves primarily with whether or not the administrator has kept within the law.[70] And this excessive judicialisation of proceedings is pushed back into the administrative stage also, thus producing a mass of hearings, written records and technical operations, accompanied by delay and expense.[71] Here again we may encounter an example of where the remedy is, for many citizens, worse than the disease. It is purely the result of good intentions. "The more closely the administrative procedures can be made to conform to judicial procedures," said an official report in the United States in 1955, "the greater the probability that justice will be obtained in the administrative process."[72] This is a well-meant remark, but it is misconceived. It is more likely that the introduction of judicial procedures will produce increased delay, costs, complication and unintelligibility without adding very much justice.[73] Fairness, openness and impartiality in administrative procedures are desirable, indeed essential, but they are not necessarily produced by the adoption of the procedures of courts.

It is well to recall the limitations of courts and judicial processes in providing remedies for maladministration. Even at their very best, their function is, although essential and irreplaceable, at the same time limited. As the writers of the leading English textbook on French administrative law

[70] Schwartz and Wade, *op. cit.*, p. 240.

[71] *Ibid.*, p. 317.

[72] Hoover Commission on the Organisation of the Executive Branch of the Government, *Report of Task Force on Legal Services and Procedures*, p. 138.

[73] The point is well made in Walter Gellhorn, *When Americans Complain* (Harvard U.P., 1966), p. 15.

remark at the conclusion of their survey: "judicial control is, of course, only one method of controlling administrative action."[74] We may leave it there, until we have considered some of the other methods, and are ready to make an appraisal of each of them.

74 Brown and Garner, *op. cit.*, p. 137.

CHAPTER 3

MINISTERS

I

THE classical remedy for maladministration in Britain is the individual responsibility of the Minister to Parliament. He is relied upon to tell the civil servants what the citizens will not stand; he brings common sense to correct the errors of bureaucratic sense. He is a British invention, and he has been exported to many countries of the Commonwealth where, to a greater or less degree he performs the same function. In contrast he does not exist in the United States, where Ministers are not members of the Congress and their responsibility lies to the President who appoints and dismisses them and not to the Congress. That is the general picture. We must consider, now, with rather more precision, what the individual responsibility of Ministers means in Britain, and thereafter how effective it is as a remedy for maladministration.[1]

Let us begin with a statement of the doctrine. One way of discovering what the rules of the constitution are in Britain is to ask what those people who are engaged in government think they are. Here is what Mr. Herbert

[1] I have found valuable the discussion of this topic in A. H. Birch, *Representative and Responsible Government* (Allen and Unwin, 1964), Chaps. 11 and 12, and in G. Marshall and G. C. Moodie, *Some Problems of the Constitution* (Hutchinson, 1959), Chap. 4.

Morrison, then in Opposition but formerly the holder of high office in the Cabinet, said in the House of Commons about ministerial responsibility: " There can be no doubt that a Minister of the Crown is responsible for all the acts of his civil servants—and all the absence of acts required. He is responsible for every stamp stuck on an envelope—if, in government departments, stamps ever are stuck on envelopes."[2] About twenty years later in another debate in the House of Commons, the then Home Secretary, Mr. Maudling, said: " A Minister takes any praise for anything good that his department does. He must take any blame for anything bad that it does." " Ministers will remain responsible for what their departments do. If their departments get things wrong, they are to be blamed in this House because their departments get them wrong. This is the fundamental point."[3]

These are wide-ranging statements. If we are to make any sense of them we must rid our minds of one or two pieces of folk-lore which, if they ever had any foundation in fact or theory, no longer apply. The first misconception is that individual ministerial responsibility means that if a civil servant makes a mistake the Minister must say—" This is my mistake. I am personally responsible for this. It was done in my name. I did it." It is true that most acts of a government department are done in the name of a Minister. Letters are written in his name. But there must in practice be a difference between acts done by a Minister and acts done in his name. There must be a difference between: " I am to blame " and " I take the blame." There is a difference, too, in the meaning of " responsibility." If a

[2] July 20, 1954. H.C.Deb., Vol. 530, 5 s., col. 1274.
[3] May 1, 1972. H.C.Deb., Vol. 836, 5 s., col. 159.

window is broken in a classroom, the headmaster can say: " Who is responsible for this broken window? " meaning " who did it? " Or he can say: " Who is responsible for conduct in this classroom? " We can begin to make some sense out of ministerial responsibility if we start by saying that it does not mean that a Minister is to regard all acts in his department as his acts, so that he has to say " I did it," and if it is an error, " I am to blame." " I am responsible to the House of Commons for the good running of my department " is not to be equated with " I am to blame for everything that goes wrong in this department." These points may seem obvious, but in fact in common speech they are not always accepted.

The second misconception which associates itself with individual ministerial responsibility is that there is only one sanction for maladministration—the resignation of the responsible Minister. And it is thought that maladministration is avoided because civil servants exert themselves to save their Minister from resignation. This notion is encouraged by the use of oratorical flourishes by Members of Parliament such as that of Mr. Morrison in the debate in the House of Commons already referred to when he said: ". . . if the House wanted anyone's head on a charger, mine was the head it should have." [4] The notion is contrary to common sense. The penalty of resignation is far too severe for most acts of maladministration. It is like saying that there is only one penalty for breaches of the law—capital punishment. If that is the position, nobody will be convicted. And if resignation is the penalty of maladministration in the department, then no official can admit to an error, or, if

[4] H.C.Deb., Vol. 530, 5 s., cols. 1276–77.

he does, no Minister can admit to it. So, in the end, the sanction becomes meaningless.

But this interpretation of individual ministerial responsibility is not only contrary to common sense and also to good administration—for mistakes cannot be admitted—but it is contrary to fact. There is no such convention or practice in modern British government. The resignation of the Minister is not required invariably when maladministration has occurred in a department, and has been admitted by the Minister to have occurred. This seems to me to have been demonstrated by Professor S. E. Finer in an article in which he analysed the resignations of Ministers in the 100 years from 1855 to 1955. These resignations were the result of complex factors; what is certain is that they did not add up to a rule requiring the resignation of the Minister on the occurrence of admitted maladministration in his department.

> ". . . In the sense in which we have been considering it, that the Minister *may be punished, through loss of office* for all the misdeeds and neglects of his civil servants which he cannot prove to have been outside all possibility of his cognisance and control, the proposition does not seem to be a rule at all. What is the compulsive element in such a " rule "? All it says (on examination) is that if the Minister is yielding, his Prime Minister unbending and his party out for blood —no matter how serious or trivial the reason—the Minister will find himself without parliamentary support. This is a statement of fact not a code." [5]

[5] " The individual responsibility of Ministers " (1956) 34 *Public Administration* 394.

And he summarises the significance of the history in the words:

"Only when there is a minority government, or in the infrequent cases where the Minister seriously alienates his own back benchers, does the issue of the individual culpability of the Minister even arise. Even then it is subject to hazards: the punishment may be avoided if the Prime Minister, whether on his own or on the Minister's initiative, makes a timely re-shuffle. Even when some charges get through the now finely woven net, and are laid at the door of a Minister, much depends on his nicety and much on the character of the Prime Minister. Brazen tenacity of office can still win a reprieve. And, in the last resort—though this happens infrequently—the resignation of the Minister may be made purely formal by re-appointment to another post soon afterwards." [6]

II

If we clear our minds of these two exaggerations about what individual ministerial responsibility may mean—that the Minister is actually himself to blame for any act of maladministration in his department, and that the only sanction for such an act is resignation of the Minister—we may begin to build up some content for the meaning of the term which is credible. As a start, let us say that the minimum which individual ministerial responsibility can mean is that a Minister alone speaks for his civil servants to the House and to his civil servants for the House, to adopt

[6] p. 393.

some words which Professor Finer has used. He is the sole channel of communication between them. That is something, and something significant. It marks the distinction between the parliamentary executive and the non-parliamentary or presidential executive as it occurs in the United States. It implies also the anonymity of civil servants, so far as the Houses of Parliament are concerned. It is sometimes referred to as answerability. The idea was expressed, with more or less precision, by the Attorney-General of the day on May 1, 1968, when he said: ". . . It is the Minister in charge of the department who is answerable to Parliament for the working of the department. The individual civil servant is, of course, not so responsible. The action of the department is action for which the department is collectively responsible and for which the Minister in charge is alone answerable to Parliament." [7]

But although the right and duty of the Minister to be the sole channel of communication to and from the House to the department is something, and something significant, it is surely clear that it is not enough. Responsibility, and indeed answerability also, convey something more than this. They convey a sense that the Minister is concerned with what the department does. He cannot content himself with being just a spokesman. He cannot shrug things off. He cannot say: "it's nothing to do with me." In simple terms he will wish, if at all possible, to defend the department; to be able to approve and win approval for what it has done; to win praise for it, to avert blame, or to admit blame if it comes to it, all on behalf of the department.

Once we reach this point, we are able now to ask the

[7] H.C. 350 of 1967–68.

question: How far must a Minister feel obliged to defend the actions of his civil servants? And how far is he obliged himself to accept blame for actions taken by or in his department? And we find that there are answers to these questions which are generally accepted by those who operate the machinery of government, and they modify the general statements about individual ministerial responsibility which I have quoted at the beginning of this chapter. An authoritative statement of the position was made in the House of Commons on July 20, 1954, by the Home Secretary, Sir David Maxwell Fyfe, in the debate on the Crichel Down affair, in which the remarks of Mr. Morrison quoted earlier were made. He laid down four propositions.[8]

1. In a case where there is an explicit order by a Minister, the Minister must protect the civil servant who has carried out his order. He takes the blame, if necessary; or he defends it.

2. Equally where the civil servant acts properly in accordance with the policy laid down by the Minister, the Minister must protect and defend him.

3. Where an official makes a mistake or causes some delay, but not on an important issue of policy and not where a claim to individual rights is seriously involved, the Minister acknowledges the mistake and *he accepts the responsibility*,[9] although he is not personally involved. He states that he will take corrective action in the department . . . He should not in these circumstances expose the official to public criticism.

4. Where action has been taken by a civil servant of

[8] H.C.Deb., Vol. 530, 5 s., cols. 1286–1287.

[9] My italics. I take it this means or includes the responsibility for putting it right, which is made explicit in the next sentence?

which the Minister disapproves and has no prior knowledge, and the conduct of the official is reprehensible, then there is no obligation on the part of the Minister to endorse what he believes to be wrong or to defend what are clearly shown to be errors of his officers. The Minister is not bound to approve of action of which he did not know or of which he disapproves. But of course he remains constitutionally responsible to Parliament for the fact that something has gone wrong and he alone can tell Parliament what has occurred and render an account of his stewardship.[10]

It is to be noted, also, that although the Minister on the occasion of this debate, Sir Thomas Dugdale, decided that it was his duty to resign and did so, he specifically repudiated the view that he was "bound to endorse the actions of officials whatever they may be, or that I or any other Minister must shield those who make errors against proper consequences."[11] There is room for argument about the propriety or necessity of his resignation, but it seems clear that he thought himself personally involved in the decisions that were taken, and that if they had gone wrong, then he must resign, whether or not he thought that the decisions he had taken were wrong.

The debate in the House of Commons on July 20, 1954, seems to me to have been of a high standard as a discussion of the constitutional implications of the notion of individual ministerial responsibility. By comparison with it, the debate in the House on May 1, 1972, on the Report of the Tribunal of Inquiry into the collapse of the Vehicle and

10 And here again "constitutionally responsible" must mean responsible for seeing that it is put right.

11 H.C.Deb., Vol. 530, 5 s., col. 1186.

General Insurance Company [12] seems rather confused and incoherent. In particular the remarks of the then Home Secretary seem at times self-contradictory and lacking in the precision that might have been expected from such a source on an occasion of this kind. But making allowance for the difference in legal training between Sir David Maxwell-Fyfe and Mr. Maudling, and for the difficulty of expressing these matters in plain and unambiguous language, the main points laid down in the debate of 1954 are re-affirmed in 1972. One or two quotations may be made. "It is no minimising of the responsibility of Ministers to Parliament to say that a Minister cannot be blamed for a mistake made, if he did not make it himself, and if he has not failed to ensure that that sort of mistake ought not to be made." [13] And, a little more positively: "If a Minister gets it wrong or fails to ensure that the other chap has not got it wrong, that Minister is to blame."

But in another passage from his speech Mr. Maudling seemed to shy away a little from these propositions. "A Minister cannot say in this House: 'I am sorry. We made a mess of it. It was not my fault. Mr. So-and-So, the assistant secretary, got it wrong that day.' One cannot do that. That has not been the principle and it never can be." Well, it would be considered very caddish to put it like that. But there could be occasions, in the situations envisaged by Sir David Maxwell-Fyfe, where the Minister could say: "I am very sorry. We got it wrong. We made a mess of it. I do not approve of what was done and have taken steps to have the matter put right and to ensure, as far as possible, that it does not occur again." He need not

[12] H.C. 133 of 1971–72.
[13] H.C.Deb., Vol. 836, 5 s., col. 159.

say: "It was my fault." He need not name the official, who may in any case by this stage have been named already by some tribunal. But it will be clear that the blame is not upon the Minister personally but somewhere in the department.

In the particular case of the Vehicle and General inquiry no Minister resigned; no action was taken by Ministers against the officials named in the report of the tribunal; and in the debate in the House of Commons, though one or two Members criticised Ministers, there was a general sympathy for the officials, no demand for punishment, but an acquiescence in the view that this was "not a resigning matter." [14]

To attempt a preliminary and brief summing-up: we can say that the individual responsibility of Ministers means, first, that they alone speak for their officials to the House, and to their officials for the House; and, secondly, that they will defend the actions of their officials, and, where they cannot, they will take the responsibility for saying that a mistake has been made and that they will take steps to see that it is put right. But "responsibility" does not require Ministers to say that *they themselves* have made the mistake, unless of course they have personally done so or authorised the doing of it or neglected to take the steps necessary to prevent such a mistake, if they could reasonably have done so.

In an odd way, one is reminded, after more than a century, of the aphorism attributed to Sir George Cornewall Lewis by Walter Bagehot: ". . . it is not the business of a Cabinet Minister to work his department. His business is to

[14] H.C.Deb., Vol. 836, 5 s., col. 122 (Mr. Nicholas Edwards, Pembroke).

see that it is properly worked." [15] Perhaps this is the sum of what individual ministerial responsibility means so far as providing a remedy for maladministration is concerned.

III

The scope of a Minister's individual responsibility seems to be summed up therefore in these two statements by Home Secretaries. Sir David Maxwell-Fyfe said in 1954: "It is part of a Minister's responsibility to Parliament to take necessary action to ensure efficiency and the proper discharge of the duties of his department. On that, only the Minister can decide what is right and just to do, and he alone can hear all sides, including the defence . . . He can lay down standing instructions to see that his policy is carried out. He can lay down rules by which it is ensured that matters of importance, of difficulty or of political danger are brought to his attention." [16] And Mr. Maudling said in 1972: "Ministers are responsible not only for their personal decisions but also for seeing that there is a system in their departments by which they are informed of important matters which arise. They are also responsible for minimising the dangers of errors and mistakes as far as possible, and, clearly, they are responsible for the general running of their departments. This is still the right doctrine of ministerial responsibility." [17]

But what does this add up to in terms of a remedy for maladministration? What, to begin with, ought we really to expect a Minister to be able to do? The first fact to

[15] *The English Constitution* (World's classics ed.), p. 200.
[16] H.C.Deb., Vol. 530, 5 s., col. 1287
[17] H.C.Deb., Vol. 836, 5 s., col. 159.

record and to realise is that a Minister can give only a very small part of his time and attention to the correction of errors of administration. He has his duties as political head of a department in dealing with policy, in discussing general issues of administration, in taking part in parliamentary and party political work in the House and in the country, in attending ministerial meetings at various levels and in visits outside the department at home and abroad. This means that, save when questions are asked in the House, or motions are moved on the adjournment, or an issue is raised otherwise in a debate, and he is obliged to explain or defend the actions of his department, his mind is not given largely to questions of maladministration. Nor should it be, in my opinion. He must rely on his officials to keep an eye on these things and to give him the necessary warnings of trouble and the material with which to answer questions, to defend what has been done or, if need be, to admit a mistake. Everything or almost everything comes back in the end to the arrangements made in the department by which officials ensure that the Minister's responsibilities are properly discharged on his behalf. Put simply, there should be a system which ensures that the Minister is kept out of trouble, so far as officials can do it.

In a sense the individual responsibility of Ministers is really in the care of the civil servants. It must be a very rare Minister who can devise a system within his department to ensure that maladministration is foreseen or prevented or remedied. He must rely on the officials at the head of his department to construct the right procedures and to see that they are applied. It is significant that, in the debate on the Vehicle and General Insurance Co. Report in the House of Commons on May 1, 1972, Mr. Douglas

Jay, himself a former president of the Board of Trade, should remark: "I cannot in a few moments lay down a clear doctrine of ministerial responsibility. Perhaps Sir William Armstrong and Sir Burke Trend will get together and try to do it for us." [18] Indeed no two people concerned with British politics and certainly no two civil servants could have a stronger belief in ministerial responsibility or a greater concern that it should operate than the Head of the Home Civil Service and the Secretary of the Cabinet. They must be even more enthusiastic in support of it than some Ministers, and their advice must be sought on occasions of doubt or where questions of constitutional propriety arise.

There are occasions when we can envisage an official thrusting a Minister's responsibility upon him, insisting that he (the official) will obey, if only the Minister will give the order. A select committee of the House of Commons was appointed in January 1972 to inquire into the circumstances in which draft parliamentary questions had been prepared in the Department of the Environment by civil servants on the instructions of the Minister for Housing and Construction for distribution to Members of Parliament on the government side of the House in an endeavour to counter a campaign of questions from the opposition side. In evidence to this committee the Head of the Home Civil Service said: "The overwhelming presumption is that a civil servant carries out the instructions of a Minister and, unless there are reasons to the contrary, that is what he does. I suppose it arises mostly in relation to ministerial powers . . . Ministers are frequently wanting to do things and it has to be pointed out to them that they do not have the powers to do them." [19]

[18] H.C.Deb., Vol. 836, 5 s., col. 119.
[19] H.C. 393 of 1971–72, pp. 19–20, Qu. 193.

He went on to illustrate the position in its extreme form by quoting from an official publication called *Government Accounting* which described the duties of the accounting officer in a department (who is, as a rule, the permanent secretary) and in particular the procedure to be followed in the event of disagreements between the accounting officers and a Minister. The paragraphs concerned are of sufficient interest, in the way in which they involve both Ministers and officials and Parliament through the Public Accounts Committee and the Comptroller and Auditor-General, to deserve quotation in full.

> " It may happen that an accounting officer disagrees with his Minister on a matter of importance affecting the efficient and economic administration of his department and thus the accounting officer's duty to Parliament. In such a case the accounting officer is expected to place on record his disagreement with any decision which he considers he would have difficulty in defending before the Public Accounts Committee as a matter of prudent administration. Having done so he must, if the Minister adheres to the decision, accept it, and, if necessary support his defence of the action taken by reference to the policy ruling of the Minister.
>
> " Alternatively the matter of the accounting officer's disagreement and his protest may be one which involves his personal accountability on a question of the safeguarding of public funds or the formal regularity or propriety of expenditure. In that case he should state in writing his objection and the reason for it and carry out the Minister's decision only on a written instruction from the Minister overruling his objection. He should

> then inform the Treasury of the circumstances and communicate the papers to the Comptroller and Auditor-General. Provided that this procedure has been followed, the Public Accounts Committee may be expected to acquit the accounting officer of any personal responsibility for the transaction." [20]

One can see that the nastiest moment for a Minister is when a civil servant says to him: " Will you order me to do this? If so, I will obey." That is individual ministerial responsibility with a vengeance.

Or we can look at another aspect of the relationship between official and Minister. When the Attorney-General of the day was giving evidence to the Committee on section 2 of the Official Secrets Act, presided over by Lord Franks, he was asked how one could be assured that in taking decisions on whether or not prosecutions under the Act should be instituted, he could rid his mind of the influence of political considerations. He replied that " if he were minded to prevent or stop a prosecution for party political beliefs, or attitudes or decisions or motives, he would be faced with a situation in which he would clearly have to make that decision in the presence of, for instance, the Legal Secretary who has been with probably Attorneys-General of a different political party before, and who on seeing the law was being distorted because a man was motivated by party political considerations would I imagine make his representations to the Secretary of the Cabinet." The Legal Secretary, said the Attorney-General, was a civil servant and as such was probably more independent than a permanent secretary in a normal department in that his duties were

[20] *Ibid.*

quasi-judicial. There was also the consideration that the Director of Public Prosecutions, also a permanent official, when faced with an obvious party political decision by an Attorney-General, would either resign or make it known that he would resign if such a situation arose.[21]

In the end it does not seem too much to say that individual ministerial responsibility at any given time and in any given situation is what the Head of the Home Civil Service and the Secretary of the Cabinet say it is. They are the keepers of the Ministers' constitutional consciences.

Mr. Douglas Jay's remarks in the Vehicle and General debate led us off into what might seem a slight digression. His next sentence may serve to bring us back. "I will only say," he continued, "that if Ministers are going to resign when anyone makes a mistake in a department, there will very soon be no Ministers left. If, on the other hand, everything is referred to Ministers, departments will rapidly grind to a stop."[22] This doctrine is certainly applied in all large departments and carried out down to a level far removed from the Ministers' knowledge. There is some interesting information about this in the Report of the Tribunal of Inquiry into the collapse of the Vehicle and General Insurance Co.

According to the Report of the Tribunal,[23] in the Department of Trade and Industry, as it was organised in 1971, the permanent secretary had the overall responsibility for the organisation and work of the Department. Ministers gave political direction to the Department's operations and piloted

[21] Committee on section 2 of the Official Secrets Act (Vol. 3, Oral Evidence, pp. 215–218).
[22] H.C.Deb., Vol. 836, 5 s., col. 119.
[23] H.C. 133 of 1971–72, paras. 61, 62.

legislation through Parliament. Once the legislation was passed and any ministerial guidance given, the officials were expected to take entire charge of the administration unless there were problems with which they needed guidance from higher up, or unless there were any other matters of particular political sensitivity about which they thought Ministers ought to know. There was a deliberate policy of delegating authority downwards. ". . . Almost all the work allocated to a division is dealt with in full and finally at the level of under-secretary or below, and that only when there is clear reason for making an exception is a matter referred higher by the under-secretary." "In dealing with the day-to-day work within the division the general arrangement is that work should be done at the lowest level at which it is practicable, so that there tends to be a filtering process from the bottom upwards, and not from the top downwards." [24]

There follows an account of the duties of an under-secretary, which, it may well be thought, could, without much adaptation, be applied also to a Minister. "It is an inherent and important part of the duties of an under-secretary, when the nature of the work requires the formulation of a policy or practice, to prescribe the policy or practice to be followed. Even when he does not involve himself in detail, a senior officer has a responsibility for supervising the work of his juniors, or for seeing that the work of his section, branch or division as a whole is well organised and proceeding efficiently. The responsibility of a senior officer does not end with matters of policy or organisation. He must exercise initiative and be prepared to enforce action when the work of junior staff has failed to produce a satis-

[24] Para. 69.

factory result or failed to resolve persisting doubts; and he must have a nose for trouble." [25]

There is a great deal to be said in favour of this organisation as a scheme. It was described by a Member of Parliament as "government by under-secretaries" [26]; it is an accurate description as far as it goes. And there is no intrinsic, inherent reason why it should not work. Within the department, it is clear where the responsibility lies, where judgment must be exercised in deciding when and what to refer upwards, and in particular when to inform or involve the Minister. At the same time it is possible to conceive a situation where, through a failure to refer matters higher up, when something went wrong the blame would rest with officials. And this is how the Tribunal on this occasion looked at the matter. The blame was placed upon an under-secretary and two assistant secretaries. Ministers and indeed all officials above the level of under-secretary were exonerated. So far as Ministers were concerned, the argument seemed to be that either they were ignorant of the whole matter, or that when they were informed of it or raised questions about it, they believed and were entitled to believe that the answers and explanations which they received were satisfactory.[27]

There is room for argument about the merits of the judgments made by the Tribunal. No evidence was taken from Ministers. The officials who were blamed were blamed for inaction, not for action, for a reluctance to use discretionary powers, not for arbitrariness.[28] Yet it was admitted that if they had acted, the insurance company would have gone into liquidation, with consequent loss, and if they

[25] Para. 70.
[26] H.C.Deb., Vol. 836, 5 s., col. 112 (Mr. Sheldon).
[27] Para. 343.
[28] Para. 166.

did not act, the same thing could happen and in fact did.[29] These and other questions were raised in the debate in the House of Commons on May 1, 1972. It was clear that most of the Members who spoke were sympathetic to the officials who had been named. The Secretary of State for the Department of Trade and Industry indicated that he had no intention of taking action against the officials, while at the same time he outlined plans for strengthening the powers of the Department to deal with insurance companies.

All these are matters for argument. What emerged from the inquiry and the discussion that followed it was that ministerial responsibility somehow seemed to play very little part in the whole matter. (It is interesting to note that, had the under-secretary who was blamed referred matters higher up, he would probably have escaped responsibility.[30]) Some Members of Parliament commented on this and asserted that if Ministers had been doing their job, they would have noticed that things were not right and taken some action.[31] One drew an extreme conclusion. Mr. Edward Gardner said: " I submit that the doctrine of ministerial responsibility in these circumstances in the light of this report can be regarded as nothing more than a myth . . . I submit that where a Minister relies on the competence of a civil servant, in whom he has with good cause complete confidence, to carry out the duties imposed by statute and gives no further instruction on his own initiative to implement or in any way to qualify the terms of the statute, and then that civil servant, acting within the confines of the trust

29 Paras. 169 and 336.

30 The point was acknowledged by the Secretary of State in the debate. H.C.Deb., Vol. 836, 5 s., col. 72.

31 *e.g.* Mr. Arthur Lewis (col. 103), Mr. Sheldon (col. 112), Mr. Edwards (col. 122), Mr. Dell (col. 127).

the Minister has in him, for one reason or another fails to come up to the standard of competence that was thought to be his, the Minister in practice, whatever may be said in theory, cannot be held to be responsible. Different considerations and different conclusions might arise if the Minister had given his own instructions on his own initiative, but in this case, and for the reasons I have submitted, the doctrine of ministerial responsibility does not apply."[32]

One small footnote to this particular affair may be added, for it helps to illustrate another well-known limitation on individual ministerial responsibility. In the period covered by the Report of the Tribunal there had been no fewer than six Ministers responsible for the subject-matter, whether as President of the Board of Trade or Secretary of State for Trade and Industry. Who, if anyone, is to be blamed? And, in particular, when the maladministration is held to consist in lack of action, who is to blame? Is it to be the Minister in office at the time of the collapse? There is no doubt about who must speak for the department in the House and to the department for the House—it is the current incumbent. But if blame is to be assigned to Ministers—and none was so assigned in the Report of the Tribunal—to whom is it to be assigned? The change of Ministers somehow provides a screen behind which individual responsibility evaporates.

IV

The notion of the Ministers as a screen behind which departmental activities are carried on, shielded from the view of Parliament and the public, is common in the dis-

[32] col. 116.

cussion of the effectiveness of individual ministerial responsibility as a remedy for maladministration. This is a criticism that can be made without any allegations of conspiracy or bad faith on the part of officials. The Minister must rely on his officials to provide him with the answers to questions in Parliament or questions and complaints in letters sent to him directly or through Members of Parliament from citizens who allege maladministration. In some matters he may show a particular personal interest but in the end he depends on his officials. It is not surprising that to the public the Minister seems identified with the department. He finds it natural to support his officials and to defend them whenever possible. Normally he owes a very great deal to them and mere gratitude, if nothing else, makes him ready to come to their aid. Indeed Ministers and officials need each other. Both are anxious to be able to show that they are running a successful department. It means, however, that in regard to the great majority of complaints of maladministration, the citizen is bound to feel that the workings of the department are concealed from him and that, with the best will in the world, the Minister will be able to do no more than repeat what an official in the department tells him.

This is not to suggest that officials are able, or feel that they are able, to get away with anything behind the screen of ministerial responsibility. Although, as I have maintained earlier, the notion that the resignation of the Minister will follow the discovery of maladministration in his department is erroneous, there are other sanctions. No department likes to acquire the reputation of being badly run—a reputation which can arise if a succession of questions and motions in Parliament and letters to the press alleging maladministration are not answered satisfactorily. Officials are anxious to give their Minister a good case with which to defend the department against criticism. And quite apart from adverse publicity in the press or in the House, officials are concerned for their own reputation and the reputation of their department within the smaller but critical world of the civil service itself. Professional pride of the official, combined with the political reputation of the Minister, go a long way to ensure that maladministration will be avoided, or, if it occurs, will be remedied through the device of individual ministerial responsibility.

But having said this, it is necessary, in order to complete the picture, to mention what limits are placed upon the use of the device of individual ministerial responsibility. There is first the limit of parliamentary time, which restricts the opportunities for ordinary oral questioning of Ministers or the raising of examples of maladministration upon motions for the adjournment of the House or similar occasions. The fact is " that the total number of questions set down for oral answer far exceeds the number for which time for an answer can be found." [33] " On present figures," said Mr. D. N. Chester, an authority on the subject, " this could be achieved only if the House were to turn itself into an almost continuous Question Time," [34] but, as he says, this is a non-starter. Yet there has been a great increase in the matters for which Ministers are accountable. Mr. Chester estimated that " if the length of Question Time had been related to an index of ministerial powers, the 50–55 minutes fixed in 1906 should now be at least four or five

[33] H.C. 393 of 1971–72, *Report from the Select Committee on Parliamentary Questions.* Evidence of Mr. C. A. S. S. Gordon, Principal Clerk of the Table Office, p. 50.

[34] *Ibid.*, p. 88, para. 9.

hours. Parliament has, however, continued to lengthen the list of things for which Ministers are accountable without accepting the implications for Question Time." [35] ". . . the House still refuses to spend even a full sixty minutes on the 'Question Hour.' " [36] As a result, in 1971, 15,107 questions were tabled in the House of Commons for oral answer and 4,907 of them, or roughly one in three, were reached.[37] Despite discussion of the problem in select committees of the House of Commons between 1959 and 1972 and the production of six reports,[38] and some attempts at reform of procedure, it is clear that the possibilities of improving the situation are very limited. Party politics have taken over Question Time; " it is now being drawn into the battle of the two front benches." [39] So that with a time restriction of fifty-five minutes on each of the days Monday to Thursday, combined with the large number of questions asked, it is clear that the check on maladministration through the parliamentary question is very limited in its application.

There is not only the restriction imposed by parliamentary time upon questioning Ministers or moving motions about matters for which Ministers are admittedly answerable and responsible. In addition to this, restrictions have come to be imposed upon the matters for which Ministers are to be held answerable and it is current government policy to experiment by extending this sphere. It is suggested that, partly as a consequence of the setting up of large departments, the detailed personal accountability of a Minister,

[35] *Ibid.*, p. 87, para. 3.
[36] *Ibid.*, p. 89, para. 11.
[37] *Ibid.*, p. vii, para. 11.
[38] H.C. 92 of 1958–59, H.C. 188 of 1964–65, H.C. 153 and H.C. 410 of 1966–67, H.C. 198 of 1969–70 and H.C. 393 of 1971–72.
[39] H.C. 393 of 1971–72, p. 89.

possible when departments are small and expenditure and staff limited, is no longer realistic. In order to make the governmental machine more manageable, attempts are being made " to separate purely executive blocks of work and to delegate them to separate accountable units of management." [40] The delegation takes two forms. One, sometimes called " hiving-off," involves transferring the work to bodies outside departments altogether. This is the case, for example, with the nationalised industries, for whose day-to-day control a Minister is not accountable, though he is accountable for major policy. The tests which may be applied for this kind of hiving-off, it is suggested, are " whether the work is of a sufficiently commercial character to enable the organisation to be regarded as wholly or largely financially self-supporting and its efficiency to be measured by the price mechanism or some other form of performance test. In addition, its responsibilities should involve little or no policy-making functions and little or no discretionary authority of a kind which might affect the liberty or rights of the citizen." And it is concluded: " if these tests are satisfied, there should be little need for ministerial accountability." [41]

In a large part of central administration, however, these tests are not met. But it is believed that " there are certain executive blocks of work where the degree of ministerial accountability can be reduced in so far as issues of policy are rarely involved and there is little need for day-to-day ministerial supervision. In such cases the government's

[40] This quotation and others that follow are from a paper by T. H. Caulcott, then an under-secretary in the Civil Service Department, published in 1973 in *Management Services* and entitled " Developments in the Organisation of Government Departments." The exposition here is based upon this paper.

[41] Para. 11.

policy is to devolve management as far as possible to officials in charge of the organisation but also to require them, subject to broad ministerial direction, to answer for the operation of the particular units involved." [42] This would be delegation to what are thought of as departmental agencies. There are plenty of problems in carrying out these forms of delegation, considered only from the point of view of principles of organisation and management. And who is answerable to whom?

This is the kind of "thinking" that found favour in the report of the Fulton Committee on the Civil Service.[43] The Committee claimed to be much impressed with what they had seen in Sweden where the principle of "hiving-off" is widely applied. Central departments deal in the main with policy making, and the task of operating and managing policies is hived off to autonomous agencies whose senior staff are mainly older men of mature experience. They recommended "an early and thorough review of the whole question." [44] And in the meantime they believed that there should be established "in departments, forms of organisation and principles of accountable management, by which individuals and branches can be held responsible for objectively measured performance." [45] And again one asks "accountable to whom"? And the answer seems to be "effectively to other officials." "These proposals entail clear delegation of responsibility and corresponding authority." [46] No doubt measures of this kind constitute one way of approaching the problem of preventing or reducing or remedying maladministration. The interesting thing about

[42] Para. 12.
[43] Cmnd. 3638, esp. paras. 188–190.
[44] Para. 190.
[45] Para. 191.
[46] Para. 281.

them is that they have in common a lack of confidence in the effectiveness or even the possibility of individual ministerial responsibility.

It is noteworthy that the semi-official paper by Mr. Caulcott from which quotations have been made remarks: "The more the Government tries to simplify its task by simultaneously amalgamating functions and delegating accountability, the more the average citizen is liable to feel that administration is becoming 'de-personalised' to an extent which diminishes his 'participation' in the process by which he is governed and may even threaten his identity as a free and equal member of a democratic society." [47]

Mr. Robert Sheldon M.P. expressed the position well in a debate in the House of Commons: "We need to ensure, through the chain from Parliament to Government, to big Minister, to little Minister and to the civil servants, a proper degree of control but it is not likely to be attained under the present arrangements. We can ensure a measure of control, however, by bringing the civil servants themselves into our select committees so that they may be asked to justify their decisions. With the greater complexity of the new system, with super-ministries, this need will become greater, not less. The questioning function is critical." [48] He was speaking in a debate about the use of select committees and it is to this subject, that, in a short time, we shall turn.

V

Just as in British central government the Minister is thought of as charged with the function, among others,

[47] Para. 13.
[48] H.C.Deb., Vol. 806, 5 s., col. 728. November 12, 1970.

to correct or prevent maladministration, so in local government it is the councillors who are thought of as the check upon bureaucracy. The machinery is very different. Instead of one man having responsibility as in central government, the responsibility in local government is vested in a many-headed body, a council or a committee, whose members are, at one and the same time, in charge of administration but also the watchdogs against maladministration. In particular the councillor, like the Member of Parliament, is expected to take up the grievances of his constituents and raise with officials or with the responsible committees or the whole council, matters in which it is alleged that maladministration has occurred.

There has been a good deal of discussion and criticism about the system by which administration is carried out in English local government. In particular it is said that more should be left to officials. ". . . members are misled into a belief that they are controlling and directing the authority when often they are only deliberating on things which are unimportant and taking decisions on matters which do not merit their attention." These were the conclusions of the Committee on the Management of Local Government under the chairmanship of Sir John Maud (later Lord Redcliffe-Maud) and they recommended in their Report [49] that committees should not be directing or controlling bodies nor should they be concerned with routine administration. There is room for a good deal of argument about the correctness of the Maud Committee's analysis of the working of the system of local government and of the wisdom of its recommendations. How far they will be carried into effect remains

[49] Para. 165 (a).

to be seen. Our particular concern is with one part only of the system, namely, the function of the councillor in bringing the grievances of his constituents to the attention of the council or its officials. This is a function which, in my opinion, councillors have performed in the past on a large scale and with considerable effectiveness. They have access to the officials and to the deciding bodies and they know the ropes. They have been valuable intermediaries between the citizens and the town or county hall. If new administrative arrangements are made in local government, and if in particular more power of decision is given to officials, the function of the councillor as critic of administration, as a sort of complaints officer or grievance man, will be even more important. Indeed, in the report of the Maud Committee, it is recognised that, if their recommendations are carried into effect, it will remain a function of the committees of councillors to " consider the interests, reactions and criticisms of the public and convey them to the officials and if necessary to the management board." [50]

Although councillors have always been associated more closely with administration and with officials in local government than Members of Parliament have been with central administration, there are some limitations on their effectiveness as critics of maladministration. To begin with, in spite of what is said about councillors concerning themselves too much with the detail of administration, there is no doubt that they find it difficult to penetrate behind the official curtain. A chairman of a committee may be able to do this to some extent, but even he must accept, as a general rule, the defence which officials make of their conduct. There is

[50] Para. 166 (c).

inevitably and naturally a closing of the ranks by officials under the pressure of critical councillors, especially if the councillors are not members of the committee concerned. There is, in addition, a feeling of loyalty to their officials by councillors who are members of the relevant committee which predisposes them to defend what has been done. None of these reactions is necessarily blameworthy. There are certain virtues of integrity in particular, which, on some occasions, officials must defend against the wishes of councillors who may hope that a rule may be waived or adjusted for the benefit of a constituent.

From the point of view of the citizen seeking redress of grievances, however, there are some further inadequacies in the existing organisation of local government, and it would seem likely that these will not grow less under the proposed new system. If a Minister tends to be thought of as a screen behind which official activities go on, a committee or a council is even more so. Actions taken in the name of a committee or a council seem even more remote than actions taken in the name of a Minister. And although a chairman of a committee may defend the actions of the committee and may indeed be a well-known local councillor and by no means faceless, there is a difference between saying " I am responsible " and " The committee is responsible." Where so many are responsible, the risk is that hardly anyone feels responsible. And behind this screen, officials proceed to take decisions and, under the proposals of the Maud Committee, will do so to a greater extent in the future.

The part-time unpaid councillor cannot be expected to devote more than a small part of his time to following up the grievances of his constituents. If he lives at some distance from the seat of government of his local authority his attention can be given to these matters only spasmodically. With the setting up of larger authorities these difficulties must be expected to increase.

Chapter 4

COMMITTEES

I

In the last chapter I quoted the statement of the Attorney-General of the time on May 1, 1968, that " it is the Minister in charge of the department, who is answerable to Parliament for the working of the department. The individual civil servant is, of course, not so responsible. The action of the department is action for which the department is collectively responsible, and for which the Minister in charge is *alone* answerable to Parliament."[1] I recall, also, the remark of the Home Secretary of the day, Sir David Maxwell-Fyfe, in the House of Commons during the debate on Crichel Down on July 20, 1954, when he said that the Minister " *alone* can tell Parliament what has occurred and render an account of his stewardship."[2] Of the remarks of the Attorney-General more will have to be said at a later stage. But his statement and that of the Home Secretary stresses once more that it is the Minister alone who speaks to Parliament for his officials and to his officials for Parliament. What the department has to say to Parliament is said by the Minister. What the department says to the Minister is screened effectively from the eyes and ears of Parliament by ministerial responsibility.

[1] To the Select Committee on the Parliamentary Commissioner for Administration. H.C. 350 of 1967–68. My italics.

[2] H.C.Deb., Vol. 530, 5 s., col. 1287. My italics.

One consequence of this doctrine or one illustration of its working is commonly thought to be the anonymity of civil servants. In what sense or to what extent is it proper to speak of the anonymity of civil servants ? It is true that civil servants do not speak and are seldom referred to by name in the debates in the Houses of Parliament. But they are far from unknown or anonymous in the Palace of Westminster. Many of them are, indeed, well known to most Members. They are in close attendance upon Ministers in the chambers of the Houses, although they sit in an area which is regarded technically as outside the chambers. They are conspicuously present in the rooms where standing committees meet for debate on Bills. Ministers can hardly move a step outside their brief without consulting their officials. The constitutional rule is kept, however, in that, while the officials are visibly present and obviously closely involved in the discussions and decisions that are occurring, they speak to the Minister and it is the Minister alone who speaks to the House or to the standing committee.

But while this is substantially a true picture so far as the Houses sitting as a whole or in standing committee are concerned, there is an interesting and important difference in the proceedings of certain select committees of the Houses. Here the rules are almost reversed. Whereas in the Houses as a whole or in standing committee only the Minister can be heard and the civil servants are silent, in the select committees it is exceptional for the Minister to attend but usual for officials to attend and speak. In certain select committees set up either regularly each session or *ad hoc* to investigate aspects of administration (including therefore maladministration) it is customary for hearings to be held to which officials from the department concerned are summoned and examined about the running of their departments. It is no exaggeration to say that they are called upon to "render an account of their stewardship," to recall the words of the Home Secretary in 1954. The reports of these committees and the evidence submitted to them, with the examination of the officials (along with non-official witnesses in some cases) are published and provide a most interesting picture of the conduct of administration. Between them they cover a wide area of the operations of central government. They are not, in fact, confined necessarily or exclusively to the consideration of past or current administration. Their interest for us, however, lies mainly in this sphere, as institutions for the discovery and remedy of maladministration. Even in this sphere, however, they act not as committees for individual grievances of citizens, but rather as watchdogs in general over the conduct of administration in a department.

To mention the names of some of the select committees set up over the past twenty years or so (some regularly appointed, others *ad hoc* or temporarily) gives an idea of the width of their range—estimates, public accounts, expenditure, Statutory Instruments, race relations, education and science, science and technology, nationalised industries, and agriculture. It is not necessary for us to go into detail in describing the work of these select committees.[3] One general remark can be made, however, which is relevant to our theme. A perusal of the reports and evidence produced by the committees qualifies considerably the statement often made that a veil of secrecy obscures the inner operations of

[3] The work of the estimates committee from 1945–65 has been described and assessed excellently by Nevill Johnson in *Parliament and Administration* (Allen & Unwin, 1966).

British government. "The argument about secrecy and our consequent ignorance of what goes on in government is weak in so far as it relates to the processes of British administration. When we speak of 'public administration,' the term 'public' has to be taken seriously."[4] And that this is so is largely due to certain select committees of the House of Commons.

The use of the legislature to investigate administration is a well-known feature of the political system in the United States and in some European countries. These committees are usually specialised in their subject-matter, in such a way that the whole range of governmental administration is divided between them. Moreover, they commonly deal not just with administration, but with legislative and policy questions as well. They possess rather more independence of the government than do British committees, particularly in the United States where there is not the degree of control over the legislature by the executive which is a feature of the British system. It is not too much to say that, unless the government is willing in Britain, the House of Commons is unlikely to be able to set up a select committee, and its powers of scrutiny and investigation will seldom, if ever, be greater than what the government feels prepared to grant.[5] To this extent there is little scope for a fruitful comparison between the select committees of the Houses in Britain

[4] Nevill Johnson, *op. cit.*, p. 11.

[5] "The most fundamentally odd and humiliating aspect," exclaimed Mr. Mackintosh M.P., in a debate on select committees in the House of Commons, "is that it is up to the government to decide how the House organises itself . . . how many committees there shall be, to lay a Green Paper and to make up their mind . . . to choose the members and chairmen and to arrange the entire procedure. Is it not time to evolve a procedure in which the House decided its own organisation?" H.C.Deb., Vol. 806, 5 s., col. 685.

which concern themselves with administration, and those committees which perform this sort of function, *inter alia*, in Europe or the United States. This sometimes leads people to believe that, because the systems are so different, there is nothing that can be learned from foreign experience in the investigation of administration by committees of the legislature. This is an exaggerated view. What can be learned is that it can be done. The methods will be different. A simple transplant can seldom be made satisfactorily. But that there is a role for parliamentary committees in the scrutiny of administration in Britain seems clear.[6] There are one or two particular aspects of this process which deserve attention as part of the general theme of remedies for maladministration.

II

There is one select committee in the British House of Commons which deserves special mention at the outset, because there are features in its organisation and operation which are of unusual interest and importance for our purpose. This is the Select Committee of Public Accounts, whose function it is to act as a remedy (or one of the remedies) against financial maladministration. Its terms of reference require it to examine "the accounts showing the appropriation of the sums granted by Parliament to meet the public expenditure and of such other accounts laid before Parliament as the Committee may think fit." These accounts appear in volumes of hundreds of pages. It is obvious that a committee of lay members of the House of Commons would find it an almost impossible task to make any sense

[6] See in particular *The Commons in Transition*, A. H. Hanson and Bernard Crick (eds.) (Fontana/Collins, 1970).

of them. The most interesting and important feature of the Public Accounts Committee is that it has a permanent official and indeed a small permanent department, independent of government, to advise it. This is the Comptroller and Auditor-General and his department, the Exchequer and Audit Department. For the first four years after the setting up of the Public Accounts Committee in 1861, it had no expert staff to assist it. But with the passing of the Exchequer and Audit Departments Act of 1866, the office of Comptroller and Auditor-General was established and since that date he has guided the Committee in its consideration of the accounts, directing their attention to the places where questions of maladministration may be thought to arise. The Comptroller and Auditor-General is thought of in practice as an officer of the House of Commons, or more properly of Parliament, though he is in fact appointed by the government. But his term of office is not, like that of a civil servant, during the pleasure of the Crown, but, like that of a judge, during good behaviour, and he is removable only on an address from both Houses of Parliament. His task is to audit accounts on behalf of the House and to report direct to the House, not to the Treasury. He is a rare, though not unique, example of an official or, more accurately, of a department set up to control other officials or departments on behalf of Parliament.

One important aspect of the office of Comptroller and Auditor-General is that he and his department act as expert advisers to the Select Committee of Public Accounts; without these officials the Committee would not be able to find its way, or know where to look or what to look for. But there is another aspect, equally important. It is the task of the Comptroller and Auditor-General and his staff to provide, on behalf of the House of Commons, a continuing check on administration, from the financial point of view. Both in the function they have to perform, and in the body on whose behalf they are working, they differ from all other departments, although their interest in checking waste and irregularity in public expenditure means that they will usually be on the same side as the Treasury. It is not surprising to find that at meetings of the Public Accounts Committee officials from the Treasury sit at one end of the horseshoe table while the Comptroller and Auditor-General and his assistants sit at the other. And as the task of audit is a continuing task, and can best be conducted in close touch with the departments concerned, part of the staff of the Comptroller and Auditor-General—which numbered about 600 in 1973—are posted to the various departments and are engaged on a continuous audit as the year's transactions proceed. They work from the inside, seeking explanations from officials in the department as required, and authorising expenditure if some doubt arises.

III

A study of the Comptroller and Auditor-General and his relation with the Public Accounts Committee brings to light two important points about methods of checking maladministration. The first is that if a select committee of the House of Commons is to be effective as a check on maladministration, it must be provided with some skilled, independent and permanent staff to guide it in its inquiries. It will not necessarily need a large staff; in one or two cases it may need hardly any.

Thus, the Select Committee on Statutory Instruments

(first set up in 1944), is able to do its work effectively with the advice of an official of the House. Its task is to consider every Statutory Instrument laid or laid in draft before the House to determine whether the special attention of the House should be called to it on certain grounds, including that it imposes a charge on the public revenues or contains provisions requiring payments to be made to the government; or that it is made in pursuance of an enactment containing specific provisions excluding it from challenge in the courts; or that it appears to make some unusual or unexpected use of the powers conferred by the statute under which it was made; or that it purports to have retrospective effect where the parent statute confers no express authority so to provide; or that there appears to have been unjustifiable delay in the publication of it or the laying of it before Parliament; or, in general, that for any special reason its form or purport calls for elucidation. This is a considerable task. There are a great many Statutory Instruments to look at. There is a good deal of technical knowledge involved. Members of a select committee cannot be expected to keep track of them. A skilled secretary and adviser is necessary. And since the setting up of this Committee it has been fortunate in always having such an adviser, and to this fact it owes some part of its effectiveness in overseeing the exercise by officials of rule-making powers. Its terms of reference clearly draw attention to ways in which it might be thought that a misuse of rule-making power could occur. From time to time the Committee summons an official to give evidence and to explain why a rule has been put forward in the way in which it has.

In the years after 1945 when the House of Commons was discussing ways in which it might, through the use of a select committee or committees, exercise control over estimates or public expenditure generally, as distinct from a post-mortem on accounts and expenditure already incurred, as carried out by the Public Accounts Committee, a constant theme in the discussion was the importance of providing any such committees with expert and independent advisers. In the outcome they were provided with the services of experienced clerks in the House of Commons, under the control of a clerk of financial committees, whose area covered both the Public Accounts Committee and the Estimates Committee. From time to time there has been criticism, sometimes from the Estimates Committee itself or from a subcommittee of it, that it needs more clerks to service it, or that it needs to be given expert and specialist assistance from outside the clerks department.[7] But, with an occasional exception, the staff has come from the staff of the Clerk of the House. The case for this system was put in 1946 by the then Clerk of the Financial Committees as follows:

> "In my view any efficient and experienced officer of the House can certainly learn (if he does not already know) his way about the Estimates and Accounts. He can acquire the information that I think a committee can properly ask him to supply them with. His duties are to know how to get the information that the Committee wants, not to conduct the inquiry for them, but to get the stuff before them and present it to them in the form in which they want it. Also he has another primary duty, and that is he is, or is supposed to be, an expert on parliamentary procedure and he has to advise them on that." [8]

7 Nevill Johnson, *op. cit.*, pp. 150 *et seq.*
8 H.C. 189–91 of 1945–46. Evidence of Capt. Diver, Qu. 4543.

These " House-trained " clerks, as he called them, acting with departmental liaison officers, could ensure that the Estimates Committee was well advised about what it should look for and that it should find what it was looking for. It could call the experts from the departments and from the Treasury before it; they would be in the witness chair, not part of the Committee's staff. This was the policy adopted for the Estimates Committee, and, although it was criticised from time to time, it was the usual pattern for about twenty years.

The Select Committee of Public Accounts and the Select Committee on Estimates were part of the machinery of the House of Commons to check financial administration. To these two select committees have been added others with the function of checking administration in other fields.[9] A select committee on nationalised industries was set up in 1955 to ensure some measure of further accountability in spite of the fact that day-to-day operations of the boards were not subject to ministerial responsibility. About ten years later, on the proposal of Mr. Crossman, Leader of the House in the Labour Government, two select committees were appointed, one to consider science and technology, the other to consider the activities in England and Wales of the Ministry of Agriculture, Fisheries and Food. The former continued to be re-appointed each session until the dissolution of the Parliament in 1970, but the latter was terminated in February 1969, and its place was taken by a select committee to consider the activities of the Department of Education and Science, and the Scottish Education Department. At the same time,

[9] I leave out of account here and in the remainder of this chapter the Select Committee on the Parliamentary Commissioner for Administration which is discussed fully in the next chapter.

in February 1969, a select committee to consider Scottish affairs was set up and in April 1969 a select committee to consider the activities of the Ministry of Overseas Development. Meanwhile in November 1968 a select committee had been set up to consider the operation of the Race Relations Act 1968 and the admission of immigrants to the United Kingdom.

When the Parliament of 1966–70 was dissolved therefore, the House was using nine select committees, each with the function, to a greater or less degree, of scrutinising administration. In addition to the traditional Select Committees of Public Accounts, Estimates, and Statutory Instruments, there were those on Nationalised Industries, Education and Science, Science and Technology, Race Relations and Immigration, Scottish Affairs, and Overseas Aid. The Committee of Public Accounts proceeded about its business in its accustomed way meeting in private and not, in practice, examining Ministers. But there were three points at least in the practice of certain of the other select committees which involved a break of some significance with the past. The first originated with the Select Committee on Estimates which was given the power in 1965 " to appoint persons with specialist knowledge for the purpose of particular inquiries, either to supply information which is not readily available or to elucidate matters of complexity within the Committee's order of reference." The House-trained clerks were still the mainstay of the Committee and its organisation, but a concession had been made, in fairly restricted terms, to the use of the expert. The Select Committee on Nationalised Industries acquired the same power, and so did some of the other committees. The second break with past practice, introduced by the Select Committee on Nationalised Industries, was that the committees, on certain occasions, took evidence from Ministers, and did not confine themselves to officials. During the session of 1968–69 Ministers gave evidence on fourteen occasions, whereas officials made 170 appearances. The third change was that the committees and their sub-committees commonly took evidence in public, both at Westminster and locally.[10]

With the election of the new Parliament in 1970, a re-examination of the use of select committees was undertaken. A Green Paper was published in October 1970,[11] and an interesting, though ill-attended debate was held in the House of Commons on November 12, 1970.[12] The details need not be discussed here, but it is worthwhile stating briefly the current situation so far as the use and methods of select committees to scrutinise administration are concerned. The Public Accounts Committee, of course, continues with its terms of reference and distinctive methods of work unchanged. The Select Committees on Statutory Instruments, on Nationalised Industries, on Science and Technology, on Race Relations and Immigration and on Scottish Affairs have been re-appointed,[13] but the Select Committees on Education and Science, and on Overseas Aid [14] have been dropped. The principal change was the transformation of the Estimates Committee into a Committee on Expenditure, so that it might

10 For an account of the working of these committees, see A. Morris M.P. (ed.), *The Growth of Parliamentary Scrutiny by Committee*, a collection of essays by Members of Parliament who had had experience on these select committees (Pergamon, 1970).

11 Cmnd. 4507 of 1970–71.

12 H.C.Deb., Vol. 806, 5 s., cols. 618 *et seq.*

13 So also has the Select Committee on the Parliamentary Commissioner for Administration, but, as I have said already, this will be dealt with fully in the next chapter.

14 Subject to a short-term appointment of a committee to examine evidence that had already been collected. Cmnd. 4507, para. 19.

focus its attention on public expenditure rather than on the supply estimates and examine a wider selection of issues arising in this field. And it was affirmed that, since this new committee, unlike the Estimates Committee, would not be barred from considering the policies behind the figures, there would be occasions when it would be appropriate for Ministers to give evidence before it as they had done before some other select committees.[15] It was envisaged also, that the Committee on Expenditure would have the same permanent status under the standing orders of the House as the Estimates Committee had enjoyed,[16] and that the Select Committees on Science and Technology, on Race Relations and Immigration, and on Scottish Affairs (and by implication those on Nationalised Industries and on Statutory Instruments) would be set up each session throughout the life of the Parliament.[17]

The question of staffing the select committees remains a subject for discussion and controversy. The contrast with the Public Accounts Committee, with its permanent, skilled and pervasive staff under the Comptroller and Auditor-General remains an outstanding feature of the operation of

15 Cmnd. 4507, para. 20.

16 It is found in Standing Order 87 in the 1972 edition as follows:

"87 (1) There shall be a select committee to be called the Expenditure Committee to consider any papers on public expenditure presented to this House and such of the estimates as may seem fit to the Committee and in particular to consider how, if at all, the policies implied in the figures of expenditure and in the estimates may be carried out more economically, and to examine the form of the papers and of the estimates presented to this House. . . .

"87 (3) The Committee has power to appoint persons with technical knowledge either to supply information which is not readily available or to elucidate matters of complexity within the Committee's order of reference.

"The Committee is to consist of 49 members; it and its subcommittees have power to sit in public."

17 Cmnd. 4507, para. 21.

the select committees. Although most committees are able now to appoint persons with specialised knowledge for the purpose of particular inquiries and make a modest use of this power, the intention is that such appointments must be confined to supplying information which is not readily available or to elucidate matters of complexity—though this need not prove a great restriction. But the bulk of the committees' work is founded on the House-trained clerks, to whose skill many tributes are paid. Where criticism arises from Members of Parliament themselves, it is founded upon a belief not that the clerks are ineffective but that there are not enough of them.[18] In the case of the Expenditure Committee, however, the need for something approaching the skill and methods of the Public Accounts Committee is sometimes called for. In the debate on November 12, 1970, Mr. Boyd-Carpenter (as he then was) said: "If the new committee is to work efficiently, then it is not just a question of giving it one or two extra clerks on the establishment of the department of the learned Clerk of the House. It involves equipping it with a real investigatory staff of its own. We are kidding ourselves if we think that a committee of very busy members of this House, with, as we know, many other commitments and obligations, sitting perhaps twice a week for a couple of hours can possibly get at what is referred to in the Green Paper as 'the reasons and policies behind the figures' unless there is a staff who can get at and work on the books and accounts of the Departments of State. They will be examining permanent secretaries and senior officials who have all the apparatus of Whitehall

[18] See, for example, the debate on November 12, 1970, H.C.Deb., Vol. 806, 5 s., col. 638 (Mr. Bottomley), col. 648 (Mr. Willey), col. 690 (Mr. Pink), cols. 652–653 (Sir H. d'Avigdor-Goldsmid).

behind them in coming before the Committee."[19] Mr. Boyd-Carpenter had had long experience of the Public Accounts Committee, part of it as chairman, and he testified " that the efficient working of such a committee is dependent on the provision of an adequate and substantial staff . . . If the Public Accounts Committee achieved any measure of success, it was due almost entirely to the fact that the necessary research work, the looking at the books, was done in advance for the Committee regularly throughout the year."[20]

But there is, so far, little firm ground upon which to decide how effective is the use of specialists as advisers to select committees, as opposed to the use of generalist clerks. One authority considers " that it is time to abandon the shibboleth of expert staffs as a remedy for the weaknesses of Parliament. . . . The best people to service the Committee are the generalists they now have."[21] In his opinion the use of part-time specialist advisers " has not led to any radical change in the manner in which committees are staffed and serviced. Essentially they have continued to depend on the overstretched resources of the Committee Office, on the competent generalists who will very often combine the secretaryship of a select committee with other duties. And on the whole there is little evidence of serious discontent by Members with this situation. This reflects the fact that it is still as hard as ever to discover what kind of specialist staffs for committees might be needed and how they would be related to the existing staffs of the House of Commons."[22] Members of Parliament ask for more staff; they are prepared

19 H.C.Deb., Vol. 806, 5 s., col. 632.
20 *Ibid.*, cols. 631–632.
21 Nevill Johnson, *op. cit.*, p. 155.
22 In A. H. Hanson and Bernard Crick (eds.) *The Commons in Transition*, p. 239. See also A. H. Hanson in *ibid.*, p. 89.

to make a modest use of specialists as advisers. But they believe that their " own standing would be significantly weakened if they came to rely on their own expert advisers on the American model. And it would probably destroy the necessary good relations with the departments if responsible civil service experts were, in effect, to be examined by non-responsible, unofficial experts. The committees should therefore obtain their expert advice from those giving evidence." [23] Members of Parliament, wrote a critic of this point of view, " are generalists—and proud of it." They have no desire for the kind of help which experts can give them. " The only case in which Parliament feels it right to intervene in this way, with expert facilities for investigation at its disposal, is in its control over the spending of public money exercised by the Public Accounts Committee. But this is because Parliament is supposed to be expert in only one thing, and that is in securing the proper expenditure of the money which it votes for public purposes." [24]

IV

It is not easy to form an opinion about the effectiveness or otherwise of select committees as a check upon maladministration. It is suggested sometimes that they are ineffective because their reports are seldom debated in the House of Commons; that when they are debated the attendance is poor [25]; and that the debates are monopolised by members of the select committee itself.[26] All these things are, roughly

[23] Michael Ryle, a senior clerk of the House of Commons, in *The Times*, April 17, 1963.

[24] Andrew Shonfield, *Modern Capitalism* (Oxford U.P., 1965) reprinted in R. A. Chapman and A. Dunsire (eds.) *Style in Administration* (Allen & Unwin, 1971), p. 407.

[25] Cmnd. 4507, para. 13.

[26] H.C.Deb., Vol. 806, 5 s., col. 668 (Mr. Morris).

speaking, true. But is it the appropriate test? Many Members of Parliament with experience of the work of select committees would not agree. "I do not regard as serious the argument that select committees produce reports which are not debated," said Mr. Sheldon. "We can regard the select committee as an end in itself. A select committee brings the civil servants before us. They can be questioned in a manner which is not possible in the House. At Question Time we have opportunity for only one supplementary question, and anyone who is at all competent knows how to avoid answering if he wishes not to answer. In a select committee on the other hand, a question can be put again and again until the answer is forthcoming, and civil servants can be forced to justify their decisions and reasoning. This, as I say, is an end in itself." [27] And Mr. William Hamilton remarked that "the important reason for having a committee is not so much the debate that results in the House from its report, but the influence that it should and does have on the government by making their civil servants and . . . the Ministers concerned come to the committees. It puts them on their mettle to justify the policy decisions that they are making." [28]

In slightly different words Mr. Willey, a very experienced Member of Parliament, said: "Inquiries by the select committees are important because they expose, or expose a little, the decision-making processes within the departments. Ministerial responsibility is a cloak for a lot of murkiness, muddle and slipshoddery within the departments. It is a good discipline that now and again a department has a select committee devoting its inquiry into a particular aspect of policy so that the department concerned has to make its reply

[27] *Ibid.*, col. 729. [28] *Ibid.*, col. 693. See also col. 684 (Mr. Mackintosh).

and analyse and look at the policy that it has been carrying out." [29] On debates, he remarked, "I do not suggest debates following all reports. We want debates only when there is sufficient general interest to justify them." [30]

Or let us approach the matter in a slightly different way. Let us ask the question: What do these select committees do which is not already done or would in any case be done by the Comptroller and Auditor-General's department or the Treasury or the Civil Service Department? Or rather what do they add to what the departments do? Do not the officials already control the officials? The short answer to this question is also I believe the best answer. They provide publicity. In their reports and minutes of evidence there is exposed to view an examination into the workings of the department and the defence of the officials of what the department has done or proposes to do. That this information seldom figures in the press and is seldom debated in Parliament does not deprive it of value. It is made known to an audience which is particularly interested and critical, namely, the civil service itself. Professional reputation whether of a department as a whole or of certain officials is affected by these reports. And those whose task it is in the civil service to foster its efficiency and good organisation must be expected to treat seriously what these committees publish. For officials to be required to appear before a select committee and give an account of their stewardship, and for their performance to be published in due course adds

[29] *Ibid.*, col. 648.

[30] *Ibid.*, col. 646. In Cmnd. 4507, Appendix A, there is a list of certain select committee reports in the sessions 1966–67, 1967–68, 1968–69 and 1969–70 and those debated in the House are marked with an asterisk. (The total is 10 out of 47. Reports of the Public Accounts, Statutory Instruments, and Parliamentary Commissioner Committees were not included.)

something to what can be accomplished by the private consultations and controversies undertaken inside the departments. Some words uttered in 1931 by the then Comptroller and Auditor-General, Sir Malcolm Ramsay, may be quoted: "Without the Public Accounts Committee I would be quite ineffective or more ineffective than I am now. They are the sanction on which it all depends." [31]

An example may illustrate the point. In a report published in February 1973 [32] the Public Accounts Committee drew attention to what it regarded as an error in the Department of Trade and Industry—the arrangements made with the firms engaged in the exploitation of North Sea gas, in that the public purse was not getting an adequate return on royalties or in taxes from these firms. No doubt these points had been taken up already by the Comptroller-General and his staff with the Department and with the Treasury and had been argued out between them. But it is something different for them to be taken up before the Public Accounts Committee and examined there and an attempt made to justify or explain to a committee of laymen what has been done, and for the proceedings and the report of the committee to be published. And it is to be noted that in this report, as in that of the Tribunal of Inquiry into the collapse of the Vehicle and General Insurance Company, officials (though not named in the Public Accounts Committee report) were criticised for not bringing matters of policy to the attention of Ministers—another example of the way in which individual ministerial responsibility has come to be regarded. But though these officials were not named, it is clear that, within civil service circles, they could be identified.

[31] H.C. 161 of 1931, Qu. 3758.
[32] H.C. 122 of 1972–73. *First Report of the Committee.*

Still, they were not named; anonymity was preserved. "Any attempt by the press to identify the particular civil servant responsible for certain actions is especially resented," writes Andrew Shonfield.[33] And it is interesting to encounter in the proceedings of select committees, occasions where members are denied the opportunity to look behind the screen. The quotation from the Attorney-General of the day, with which I began this chapter, was part of an appearance he made before a select committee of the House of Commons with the express purpose of telling them that they should not seek to summon before them a named official of the Foreign Office. The actions of the department, he said, are actions for which the department is collectively responsible, and for which the Minister in charge is alone answerable to Parliament. The individual civil servant is, of course, not so responsible, he said. So there is the responsible Minister, and behind him is the department, and behind it is the permanent secretary and such other spokesmen for the department as the department decides, and it is to these persons that questions from members of select committees are to be directed. "I submit," said the Attorney-General, "that it is a corollary of the principle that it is the Minister alone who is responsible for the actions of his department that the individual civil servant who has contributed to the collective decision of the department should remain anonymous."[34] And the practice of the Public Accounts Committee was commended. ". . . If you were to follow the procedure of the Public Accounts Committee in summoning the head of a department, or

[33] *Modern Capitalism*, reprinted in Chapman and Dunsire (eds.), *op. cit.*, p. 410.

[34] H.C. 350 of 1967–68, p. 73, Qu. 546.

anyone he chooses to nominate, and pursuing with him whatever matters affecting the department you think it right to pursue, that is how it would be most appropriate for you to proceed." [35]

The responsibility of the Foreign Secretary was invoked. He expressed the earnest hope that references to the official by name together with the statements attributed to him will be removed from any record or report which the select committee intends to publish.[36] The Head of the Home Civil Service, Sir William Armstrong, added his authority to the case. In his opinion the people a select committee should see are "the people responsible for the administrative systems of the department. That will in most departments be the permanent secretary of the department. There may well be cases where a department is multifarious and it has a whole branch which is concerned with one particular thing . . . If there was a branch of administration that was separate in that sense, then with the agreement of the permanent secretary—I do not think he would have any difficulty in agreeing—he would be the man to see. But what I am suggesting is that the man you should see is the man responsible for designing and laying down the administrative procedures and systems and insuring that they work rather than somebody who is simply receiving them from on high and doing his best to work them . . ." [37]

The battle was courteously conducted. It ended in a draw. The official did not appear before the select committee; references to him were deleted from the minutes of

[35] *Ibid.*, p. 75, Qu. 551.
[36] *Ibid.*, p. 70, Qu. 546.
[37] *Ibid.*, p. 105, Qu. 654.

evidence.[38] But the select committee in its report asserted that it did " not agree with the suggestion that they should confine themselves to taking evidence from the principal officer of a department where they are considering what a department should do to remedy administrative defects disclosed by the committee's investigation . . . They have an undoubted right under their Order of Reference to call for evidence from any persons who they think can assist them in their inquiry. They agree that generally the appropriate witness will be the principal officer, in view of his responsibility and authority for the administrative systems of the department with which they are concerned. On the other hand, there may well be infrequent occasions when your committee will find it necessary to inform themselves about the nature of the defect in the system as well as the measures taken to remedy the defect. For that and other purposes they may need to obtain the evidence of those officials who are concerned at first hand with the actions in question. Your committee are satisfied that they will be able to take evidence from subordinate officials for this purpose without exposing them to unfair publicity and criticism, and they feel that they can rely on departments to indicate the appropriate witnesses." [39] And they threw in one or two references to the Fulton Committee's Report of 1968 [40] which had recommended that the convention of anonymity of civil servants should be modified so that they might be able to go further in explaining what their departments were doing, and which had envisaged, in the relations between the civil service and

38 H.C. 258 of 1967–68. First Report of the Select Committee, pp. x, xi and xiii. In Minutes of evidence, p. 70, there is a gap between questions 438 and 445.
39 H.C. 350 of 1967–68, p. xii.
40 Cmnd. 3638.

Parliament, a greater involvement of officials below the level of permanent secretary.

Another illustration of the way in which the screen comes down may be quoted from the proceedings of the same committee about four years later, and on this occasion the argument is not about who shall appear as a witness but what a witness, indeed a permanent secretary, is prepared to say in evidence. A small piece of dialogue between Dame Irene Ward M.P., and Dame Mildred Riddelsdell, second permanent secretary of the Department of Health and Social Security runs as follows.[41] They are discussing why the Department had decided not to pay compensation to a citizen who felt aggrieved.

Dame Irene Ward:

> "It was not because of disapproval on the part of the Treasury?"

Dame Mildred Riddelsdell:

> "It was a straightforward judgment of where the principle of the thing lay."

Dame Irene:

> "It was never put up to the Secretary of State or even to the Treasury?"

Dame Mildred:

> "Everything we do, we do in the name of the Secretary of State."

Dame Irene:

> "That is quite a different matter, if I may say so . . . But this kind of thing you have not put up to the Secretary of State and the Secretary of State has not

[41] H.C. 334 of 1971–72, p. 30, Qu. 199–201.

even asked the Treasury whether it would think it fair to make a payment of some kind in compensation? "

Dame Mildred:

" Mr. Chairman, I think I would be going outside my constitutional brief if I discussed what advice civil servants gave to Ministers or what questions they put to them as individual questions."

Mr. Fletcher-Cooke M.P. (in the chair):

" I think it might arise in some cases, but I feel it probably does not arise here, if I may say so, because there is no suggestion that the Secretary of State disagreed with the decision of the Department not to make amends in this way."

Dame Irene:

" But he probably knew nothing about it."

And there it rested.

V

Is it, then, never possible to penetrate behind the curtain? The answer is that it is in exceptional cases. There are occasions when a committee or tribunal is set up to investigate some matter in which Ministers or officials or both are involved and where serious allegations of maladministration or improper conduct are put forward. It is usual, with these investigations, for the inquiry to go behind the scenes and to take and publish evidence from officials and Ministers, as well as others concerned, and identify persons by name and to award praise or blame according to their judgment.

Inquiries of this kind are of a different nature from those conducted by select committees of the House of Commons for they are charged with investigating particular allegations of misconduct of considerable public importance and interest with which particular people are thought to be associated. But at one time select committees were used to make these inquiries, being appointed *ad hoc* for the purpose. This was the method adopted to investigate what was known as the Marconi Scandal in 1912. Under the Liberal Government, the Postmaster-General accepted a tender from the English Marconi Company to construct a chain of wireless telegraph stations throughout the Empire and thereupon rumours circulated that the government had corruptly favoured the Marconi Company and that certain leading members of the government had profited improperly from the transaction. The select committee of inquiry was composed on party lines, with a Liberal majority; it divided in its report on party lines, with the Liberal majority exonerating the members of the government concerned and the Conservatives finding them guilty of gross impropriety; and in due course the House of Commons divided similarly and exonerated the Ministers from all blame. After this experience, it was thought unsatisfactory that allegations of maladministration of this kind, in which a party political element was likely to be involved, should be investigated by a select committee inevitably composed on party lines, and indeed the inquiry into the Marconi Scandal is the last case of a matter of this kind being investigated by a select committee of Parliament. Instead it is customary now, though not invariably so, to appoint a tribunal under the Tribunals of Inquiry (Evidence) Act of 1921.[42] The hearings are held in public as a general rule, though there is a power to exclude the public if the tribunal is of the opinion that " it is in the public interest so

[42] 11 Geo. 5, c. 7.

to do for reasons connected with the subject-matter of the inquiry or the nature of the evidence to be given." The report and evidence are published.

The working of the Act of 1921 has been examined by an authoritative Royal Commission under the chairmanship of Lord Justice (later Lord) Salmon which reported in November 1966 [43] and which was concerned particularly with safeguarding persons who were called to give evidence before a tribunal, and also persons who may otherwise be interested in the subject-matter of the inquiry. The Royal Commission laid down six cardinal principles the observance of which would go some way to removing the difficulties and injustice to which persons involved in an inquiry might be subject. Our interest in the subject, however, is merely to note that by the use of a tribunal of inquiry under the Act of 1921 or of some similar procedure, the curtain which hides from public view what goes on in government departments is, partially and temporarily at any rate, drawn aside and the workings of a department or part of it are revealed. Of the inquiries held under the Act of 1921 [44] some in particular were notable in this respect—that in 1936 under the chairmanship of Mr. Justice (later Lord) Porter concerning the unauthorised disclosure of information relating to the Budget in which Mr. J. H. Thomas and Sir Alfred Butt M.P. were involved [45]; that in 1948 under the chairmanship of Mr. Justice Lynskey concerning allegations of bribery of Ministers of the Crown or other public servants in connection with the granting of licences [46]; that in 1957 under the chairmanship of

[43] Cmnd. 3121 together with a volume of documentary evidence and a volume of minutes of oral evidence.

[44] For a list up to 1966, see Cmnd. 3121, Appendix C.

[45] Cmd. 5184.

[46] Cmd. 7616.

Lord Justice Parker (later Lord Chief Justice) into allegations of improper disclosure of information relating to the raising of the Bank Rate [47]; that in 1962 under the chairmanship of Lord Radcliffe into the circumstances in which offences under the Official Secrets Act were committed by William Vassall; and that in 1971 under the chairmanship of Mr. Justice (later Lord Justice) James concerning certain issues in relation to the circumstances leading up to the cessation of trading by the Vehicle and General Insurance Company.[48]

To this group of tribunals whose reports and evidence shed light on the working of government departments in an exceptional degree should be added one which was not in fact set up by both Houses under the Act of 1921 but was in fact set up by a Minister, Sir Thomas Dugdale, the Minister of Agriculture, who in 1953 appointed Sir Andrew Clark Q.C. to inquire into the disposal of land at Crichel Down. His report was published in June 1954 [49]; at a debate in the House of Commons on July 20, 1954, the Minister announced his resignation; the next day the two parliamentary secretaries offered their resignations but withdrew them at the request of the Prime Minister; and the position of the five officials chiefly concerned was considered by a committee presided over by Sir John Woods, formerly permanent secretary to the Board of Trade.[50]

47 Cmnd. 350.

48 H.C. 133 of 1971–72. This tribunal and that of Lord Widgery into the events of " Bloody Sunday " in Londonderry, sat after the report of the Salmon Commission and it should be added to the list of tribunals in Appendix C of Cmnd. 3121.

49 Cmd. 9176.

50 Cmd. 9220. One was transferred to other duties. No further action was recommended on the other four, in two cases because they had already been transferred.

The Crichel Down affair was a very complicated matter. A classic account of it was published by D. N. Chester [51] who appraises its significance, in relation, among other things, to maladministration, in a masterly manner. In our discussion of individual ministerial responsibility in the previous chapter, we have mentioned the debate in the House of Commons on July 20, 1954, and the comments made by the Home Secretary on the implications of the case for the relationship of a Minister and his civil servants. But it is in connection with the penetration behind the anonymity of the civil servant that the Crichel Down inquiry is historic. "Civil servants had never before been the subject of an inquiry where they had publicly to explain their actions." [52] It was not, of course, the first time that Ministers, departments (even the Ministry of Agriculture) and civil servants had been in error, as Mr. Chester points out. The reports of the Public Accounts Committee always contain a few examples. "But even the Public Accounts Committee, though it examines leading departmental officials and publishes its proceedings, does not set out to ascribe praise or blame to individuals and only occasionally names an official in its critical comments." [53]

In a succinct passage which deserves quotation in full, Mr. Chester puts the Crichel Down case in perspective:

> "The significant feature of the Crichel Down case is that it brought into question not a department or a vague corporate body, nor a Minister as the political head of a department from which he receives anonymous

[51] (1954) 32 *Public Administration*, 389.
[52] R. A. Chapman and A. Dunsire (eds.) *Style in British Public Administration*, p. 360.
[53] (1954) 32 *Public Administration*, 391.

advice, but the actions of individual civil servants. These individuals had to give evidence and be examined in public and their files and correspondence were open to Sir Andrew Clark. The six volumes of evidence and much correspondence were available to Members in the Library of the House of Commons. The whole of the administrative process and the parts played by a dozen or more civil servants were subjected to minute scrutiny . . . This is the first occasion possibly since the Sadler-Morant dispute of 1903 (a comparatively minor affair) on which the whole of the administrative paraphernalia has been so treated and made public, the share of named civil servants in that process analysed and appraised and their names and actions discussed and criticised in public." [54]

In 1972 another report of comparable significance was published as the result of the inquiry already mentioned into the Vehicle and General Insurance Company's failure. Here again the whole of the administrative process and the parts played by civil servants in it were subjected to minute scrutiny. Many civil servants were named, blame was allotted, not to mention praise and faint praise also. One named under-secretary's conduct was described as falling far below the standard of competence which he ought to have displayed and it was judged to constitute negligence. He "failed to guide or control the Insurance Branch of the Department in its dealings with the company. He did not display initiative or imagination in considering the Company's affairs. The ultimate responsibility for the failure of the Department to take action against the Company lies

[54] *Ibid.*, pp. 390–391.

with him."[55] Two other named officials were judged by the Tribunal to deserve criticism, but their conduct did not amount to negligence. And another named official in a minor post was judged guilty of "misconduct," by which the Tribunal understood "a deliberate dereliction of duty on the part of a person who knows that he is acting wrongfully and in breach of duty."[56] It was a severe criticism of certain civil servants; there was no shield of anonymity. Nor was any blame attached to Ministers.[57] The report was debated within the House of Commons[58] and outside,[59] and there was a good deal of questioning whether justice had been done all round.[60]

But it must be emphasised that this public scrutiny of the administrative process and the part played in it by civil servants is extremely rare. Tribunals of inquiry under the Act of 1921, or indeed a departmental inquiry such as that into Crichel Down must be regarded as an exceptional remedy for suspected maladministration. They must be used as the medicine of public administration, not as its daily bread. They should not be used for matters of local or minor importance, but "confined to circumstances which occasion a nation-wide crisis of confidence" as the Salmon Report asserts.[61] As a rule some political over-tones will be found

55 H.C. 133 of 1971–72, para. 341.

56 *Ibid.*, para. 316.

57 *Ibid.*, para. 342.

58 H.C.Deb., Vol. 836, 5 s.

59 See *e.g. Political Quarterly*, 43, No. 3 for articles by R. J.-S. Baker, "The V. and G. Affair" and Lewis A. Gunn, "Politicians and Officials: Who is answerable?"

60 It may be mentioned that the Salmon Commission's Report of 1966 including the six principles had not been implemented at that date. It was announced in 1973 that legislation to carry out the recommendations was to be introduced. Cmnd. 5313.

61 Cmnd. 3121, para. 27.

in the background, if nowhere else, and the alleged responsibilities for maladministration will be confused among politicians and civil servants.

While, therefore, such inquiries are essential exceptionally, we cannot regard them as part of the regular and continuing machinery for preventing or remedying maladministration. Must we reconcile ourselves then, to occasional glimpses behind the curtain only when scandalous episodes occur? Must we be content with what select committees are able to discover for us, subject to the benevolent discretion of the Head of the Home Civil Service? Before we can answer this question finally, we should look at one other institution for remedying maladministration which has been developed in British government in recent years.

Chapter 5

OMBUDSMEN

I

Let us return for a moment to the Public Accounts Committee and the Comptroller and Auditor-General and his department. What was unique about these institutions in the context of checking maladministration was, as we saw, that the Public Accounts Committee was provided with a skilled staff to guide it in its work and, secondly, that this staff was located where necessary within the departments themselves, engaged in an internal and continuous, and to a large extent, preventive check on maladministration. The members of the Public Accounts Committee themselves might seldom be permitted to go behind the curtain of senior departmental officials, but their officers did so and reported to them.

But the significance of the Public Accounts Committee and the Comptroller and Auditor-General and their relationship with each other is even greater than this unique contribution to the checking of maladministration. For it has been substantially on this model that, when it was finally decided in Britain that an experiment should be made with some further machinery for the redress of grievances, the office of Parliamentary Commissioner for Administration was established in 1967. From the outset of the campaign to improve remedies for maladministration, the analogy of the

Comptroller and Auditor-General was used. Professor F. H. Lawson, in a short memorandum published in *Public Law* in 1957—a memorandum which was to prove most influential in initiating action as it turned out—proposed that an Inspector-General of Administration should be appointed to investigate complaints of maladministration, that he should have the same status and tenure as the Comptroller and Auditor-General, and that like him he should report to a select committee of the House of Commons similar to the Public Accounts Committee. He contemplated that the person appointed would, " like the Comptroller and Auditor-General, almost inevitably be a higher civil servant nearing the end of his career," and as such, " he would, while preserving impartiality and independence, not only have experience of administration, but be able to speak to officials and departments as one of themselves."

It is not necessary to tell here the story of the movement as a result of which the office of Parliamentary Commissioner for Administration was established in Britain and the select committee of the House of Commons on the Parliamentary Commissioner set up to work in association with him.[1] The main point is that the analogy of the Comptroller and Auditor-General and of the Public Accounts Committee was followed, so that in a fascinating way this new office, the setting-up of which owed a great deal to the public interest aroused by the institution of the Ombudsman or its equivalent in Sweden, Norway, Denmark and Finland, was, in fact, in the end, made to appear like an extension into a new field of a pair of old and tried British institutions. And to add verisimilitude to the picture, the first holder of the office

[1] The story is told in detail in Frank Stacey, *The British Ombudsman* (Oxford, 1971).

of Parliamentary Commissioner in Britain was Sir Edmund Compton, who, at the time of his appointment, was Comptroller and Auditor-General.

II

The case for establishing the Parliamentary Commissioner for Administration rests upon the assertion that there was in Britain a gap in the arrangements that existed for redressing grievances or remedying maladministration. The nature of the gap is apparent from the discussion in the preceding three chapters; some complaints of maladministration can be referred to the ordinary courts; some can be referred to tribunals set up under statute; some can be referred to a Minister after a special procedure, sometimes involving an inquiry, has been followed. These remedies were discussed in Chapter 2. "But," to quote some words from the Report in 1957 of the Franks Committee on Administrative Tribunals and Inquiries, "over most of the field of public administration no formal procedure is provided for objecting or deciding on objections. For example, when foreign currency or a scarce commodity such as petrol or coal is rationed or allocated, there is no other body to which an individual applicant can appeal if the responsible administrative authority decides to allow him less than he has requested. Of course the aggrieved individual can always complain to the appropriate administrative authority, to his Member of Parliament, to a representative organisation or to the press. But there is no formal procedure on which he can insist. . . . It may be thought that in these cases the individual is less protected against unfair or wrong decisions.

But we are not asked to go into questions of maladministration which may arise in such cases." [2]

There were then, objections by or through a Member of Parliament, who might ask a question in the House or write a letter to the department, or raise a matter in the course of a debate or on a motion for the adjournment of the House. These weapons were not useless; it is important not to exaggerate their limitations. Questions in Parliament, in spite of restrictions on their numbers and the chance of getting an oral answer, are taken very seriously in a department. Complaints raised by Members of Parliament on behalf of their constituents by letter or in person are not brushed aside. But this procedure has two inherent weaknesses. " First, the investigation is carried out by the department whose conduct is impugned and, secondly, it is based upon documents which are not available to the complainant or indeed to anyone other than the department." [3] There should be supplementary machinery to enable a Member of Parliament to secure an impartial investigation of complaints of this character if he wishes.[4]

So far as adjournment debates are concerned, the competition among Members for the use of them, a mere half-hour at the end of the day's business, is very great; the likelihood of publicity is small at that hour; and the debate tends to be little more than a restatement by each side of the grievance and the reason why it cannot be remedied. Once more there is that lack of impartial inquiry and that inability to see the documents which has already been mentioned.

[2] Cmnd. 218 of 1956–57, paras. 10 and 14.

[3] *The Citizen and the Administration*, para. 82. A report by JUSTICE, under the direction of Sir John Whyatt, and commonly called the Whyatt Report (Stevens, 1961).

[4] *Ibid.*, para. 84.

These methods of dealing with maladministration have been discussed already in Chapter 3 and group themselves under the general heading of the individual responsibility of the Minister. But as we saw in Chapter 4 they do not exhaust the opportunities open to Members of Parliament to examine the work of departments for, by the use of select committees, officials can be examined, particularly in the spheres of finance, and questions of maladministration can be raised. In the select committees it would be rare, however, for the grievance of an individual citizen to be raised. Indeed it would seldom be in order. What is dealt with are matters affecting all citizens as taxpayers or as recipients of services from the administration. Such select committees as those on public accounts, estimates, expenditure, nationalised industries and Statutory Instruments are certainly part of the machinery for preventing maladministration, but their terms of reference do not, as a rule, cover the grievance of the individual citizen.

So far as *ad hoc* inquiries are concerned, whether set up under the Tribunals of Inquiry (Evidence) Act of 1921, or by a Minister, their value, as we have just seen, is undoubted but their use must be limited. They may be needed to deal with a charge of maladministration in which great public interest or disquiet is involved, in which political figures, as well as officials, are concerned, and in which a public hearing may be essential. But they do not offer " any solution to the problem of providing a ready means of dealing with complaints of maladministration of less importance but more frequent occurrence." [5]

These methods of checking maladministration, then—

[5] Whyatt Report, para. 91.

courts and tribunals, the individual Minister's responsibility in Parliament, the examination of officials by select committees, or by *ad hoc* tribunals and so on—all play a part and usually an effective part, as remedies for maladministration. They may require improvement, amendment, strengthening. But in general, if they did not exist, they ought to be invented. But what they need is to be supplemented by an institution for investigation into complaints which is independent and thorough, which can go behind the screen which hides the department from the citizen, and from the Member of Parliament also, but which at the same time will involve the House of Commons in its historic role as a committee of grievances. And it was to fill this gap, and to perform this function, that the office of Parliamentary Commissioner for Administration and the select committee of the House of Commons to work in association with him, were set up in 1967.

III

A short statement of the position and powers of the British Parliamentary Commissioner as set out in the statute which established the office is needed at this point.

The Parliamentary Commissioner for the investigation of administrative action taken on behalf of the Crown, is like the Comptroller and Auditor-General, appointed by the Crown by Letters Patent, holds office during good behaviour (as distinct from pleasure) and may be removed by an address from both Houses of Parliament. He has the power to investigate any action taken by, or on behalf of, a government department, or other authority to which the Act applies, in any case where a complaint has been made by a member of the public, through a member of the House of Commons, who claims to have sustained injustice in consequence of maladministration in connection with the act taken. The complaint must have been referred to the Commissioner by the member with the consent of the complainant, with a request for investigation.[6]

Then follows certain restrictions on the area within which the Commissioner can investigate. In Schedule 2 to the Act there is a list of departments which may be investigated, and the Commissioner may not go outside that list. It is a long list. Its extent may be gauged by saying that it includes most of the important departments of central government, whose action impinges on the public, resident in Britain. It does not extend to local government, nationalised industries, the health service, the courts, the armed or civil services of the Crown, or the police.[7]

Next there is a general restriction to the effect that the Commissioner shall not investigate any complaint in regard to any action in respect to which the person aggrieved has a right of appeal, reference or review to a tribunal, or has a remedy by way of proceedings in a court of law. But this restriction is qualified by a provision, that the Commissioner may, in the exercise of his discretion, conduct an investigation if he is satisfied that, in the particular circumstances, it was not reasonable to expect the complainant to resort to this remedy.[8] The Commissioner has a discretion also in deciding whether to initiate, continue or discontinue an investigation of a complaint duly made to him under the Act. A complaint cannot be made by a local authority, or a

[6] 1967, c. 13, s. 5.
[7] Sched. 3.
[8] s. 5 (2).

nationalised industry or any other body appointed by the government or mainly financed by it.[9]

And, finally, the Act lays down some rules about the conduct of investigations. They must be in private. The principal officer of the department, the action of which is objected to, and any other person involved in the action complained of, must be given an opportunity to comment on the allegations. The Commissioner is free to conduct the investigation as he sees fit, to seek information and make inquiries as he thinks fit, and to decide whether persons should be legally represented, and to allow expenses to those who have complained or have assisted in the conduct of the investigation.[10] The Commissioner is given power to require any Minister or official of a department concerned to produce any relevant information which he requires, without any claim to Crown privilege. His powers exceed those of the courts in this respect. The only restriction relates to information relating to proceedings of the Cabinet, or any committee of the Cabinet, certified as such by the Secretary of the Cabinet with the approval of the Prime Minister.[11] But there is a restriction upon the Commissioner's power to publish documents or information concerning which a Minister has given notice to the Commissioner that it is his opinion that disclosure would be prejudicial to the safety of the state, or otherwise contrary to the public interest.[12] The restriction here, be it noticed, is not on the Commissioner's seeing this information and these documents, and

[9] s 6.
[10] s. 7.
[11] s. 8.
[12] s. 11.

founding his judgment on them, but on publishing or disclosing them.[13]

In the last stage of the investigation the Commissioner sends a report to the Member of Parliament who referred the complaint to him and to the principal officer of the department concerned. Further, if, after he has conducted an investigation, the Commissioner comes to the conclusion that injustice has been caused by maladministration, but that this injustice is not being, or is not likely to be, remedied by the department, he can lay a special report before each House of Parliament. He is required to lay an annual report before each House also, and may, as he thinks fit, lay other special reports before each House.[14]

The Parliamentary Commissioner Act came into force on April 1, 1967, and the Parliamentary Commissioner for Administration took up his duties. There was no reference in the Act, of course, to the select committee. That was to be set up separately by the House of Commons, session by session, and it was first appointed on November 23, 1967. Its terms of reference then and subsequently were "to examine the reports laid before this House by the Parliamentary Commissioner for Administration and matters in connection therewith."

IV

The setting up of the office of Parliamentary Commissioner

[13] In the first five years of the Parliamentary Commissioner's existence, only one such case occurred. In 1971 the Commissioners of Inland Revenue gave notice to the Parliamentary Commissioner that disclosure, without consent, of information or documents in a particular case, would be a breach of confidentiality which the Inland Revenue promises, and for that reason contrary to the public interest. H.C. 334 of 1971–72, p. vi and H.C. 116 of 1971–72, paras. 18–21.

[14] s. 10.

is an extension and adaptation of methods of preventing maladministration already established in Britain with the Comptroller and Auditor-General and the Public Accounts Committee.[15] It can be regarded legitimately as one more example of British ingenuity or flexibility in devising political institutions. But it is well known that in the campaign that preceded the decision of the Government in 1966 to introduce the Parliamentary Commissioner Bill, a great deal of reference was made to institutions in other countries where, it was asserted, remedies against maladministration were available which filled the gap about which concern was being expressed in Britain. It is interesting to notice briefly how the Parliamentary Commissioner compares with these other institutions, particularly in the extent of his powers.

Complaints may be referred to the British Parliamentary Commissioner only by members of the House of Commons; he may not receive them direct from members of the public. No such restriction applies to the New Zealand Parliamentary Commissioner[16]—an officer who operates in a parliamentary system similar to the British—who may receive complaints from any member of the public. The same is true of the Ombudsman in Sweden and in Denmark and in Norway. What is more, the Ombudsman in each of these Scandinavian countries may himself initiate an investigation if he thinks it proper to do so.

The British Parliamentary Commissioner is confined to looking at injustice arising from maladministration. In New Zealand the Parliamentary Commissioner has a wider

15 This was asserted by the government in their White Paper of 1965, Cmnd. 2767, para. 4.

16 He took up his duties on October 1, 1962, so that there had been more than four years' experience of the operation of the office before the British Commissioner took up his office.

scope—he can report on " unreasonable " actions by government departments. But it seems likely that " maladministration " as interpreted in Britain comes near to being equated with what is covered by the Swedish, Danish or Norwegian Ombudsmen, though the action which the Ombudsman may take if he finds maladministration differs from one country to another.

There are certain areas from which the British Parliamentary Commissioner is excluded—local government, the armed and civil services, the health service, to name a few. These exclusions apply to the New Zealand Parliamentary Commissioner also, with one exception, personnel matters in the civil service. In Sweden, however, the Ombudsman is not excluded from these areas. The British Parliamentary Commissioner may not investigate complaints against the police; the Ombudsmen in Sweden, Finland, Denmark, New Zealand and Norway may do so. In Sweden and Finland, also, the Ombudsman may investigate complaints against the behaviour of judges.[17]

There is one key issue upon which it is interesting to compare the position and powers of the British Parliamentary Commissioner with those of Ombudsmen or their equivalents in other countries, and this is in the sphere of discretionary power. The position is set out in the Whyatt Report and seems to be as follows: in Sweden the Ombudsman will not take up cases complaining of the way in which a civil servant has exercised his discretion unless it appears that the discretion has been so abused as not to amount to an exercise of discretion at all. (This exception is not

[17] The Norwegian Ombudsman is excluded from the area of local government.

generally realised in this country.[18]) The position seems to be much the same in Denmark. If there has been an arbitrary or unreasonable use of power, then the discretion has lost its true character. Otherwise he is not prepared merely to substitute his decision for that of the administrator.[19] The same is true in Norway.[20]

The position in Britain is governed by section 12 (3) of the Parliamentary Commissioner Act which declares that " nothing in this Act authorises or requires the Commissioner to question the merits of a decision taken without maladministration by a government department or other authority in the exercise of a discretion vested in that department or authority." In the first report which he made to Parliament, the Commissioner explained how he had interpreted his duty under this subsection so far. His practice, he said, " is to regard the area for my investigation to be the administrative processes attendant on the discretionary decision; collection of the evidence on which the decision was taken, the presentation of the case to the Minister, and so on. If I find there has been a defect in these processes, detrimental to the complainant, then I do inquire into the prospects of a remedy by way of review of the decision. But if I find no such defect, then I do not regard myself as competent to question the quality of the decision, even if, in an extreme case, it has resulted in manifest hardship to the complainant." [21] But having said this, the Commissioner concluded his report by saying that the distinctions between the quality of the procedures attending the decision and

18 Whyatt Report, pp. 49–50, para. 103.
19 Para. 115. Frank Stacey, *op. cit.*, pp. 24–25, questions this interpretation.
20 Para. 132.
21 H.C. 6 of 1967–68, para. 35.

the quality of the decision itself were difficult to draw and far from satisfactory to those who complained, and he invited the Select Committee on the Parliamentary Commissioner to advise him on the application of what he described as "the central provisions of the Act." [22]

It is interesting to see with what readiness the select committee urged the Commissioner to interpret his powers in a wider sense. After examining a number of departmental witnesses, they recommended in their report that, while they were not encouraging the Commissioner to substitute his decision for that of the government, they thought "that if he finds a decision which, judged by its effect upon the aggrieved person, appears to him to be thoroughly bad in quality, he might infer from the quality of the decision itself that there had been an element of maladministration in the taking of it, and ask for its review." [23] And the Commissioner, in his first report in the next session, 1968–69, stated that he was acting on this recommendation.[24] Geoffrey Marshall commented on this: ". . . it is, it seems, now permissible to infer that if a decision has no merits at all, there *must* have been maladministration in the way it was reached. Thus the stuffing is knocked out of section 12 of the 1967 Act, as it always deserved to be." [25] But his criticism was qualified by the remark (made in an essay published in 1970) that "in a number of cases the difference between the old and the new approach is hard to see and the Commissioner seems on the face of it still to be fighting shy of the quality and the merits of the decision." [26] The successor to Sir Edmund Compton as Parliamentary Com-

[22] Para. 38.
[23] H.C. 350 of 1967–68, p. viii, para. 14.
[24] H.C. 9 of 1968–69.
[25] Hanson and Crick (eds.) *The Commons in Transition,* p. 123.
[26] *Ibid.*, p. 127.

missioner, Sir Alan Marre, indicated to the select committee that he was prepared to follow their recommendation as his predecessor had done. He appears to act with the same caution, reinforcing himself to some extent by quoting the committee's own recommendation that "such cases will be and should be rare and that it will be a matter of judgment in individual cases."[27]

The select committee also encouraged the Commissioner to examine departmental rules and, if he came to the conclusion that they caused injustice, to feel entitled to draw the attention of the department to them and ask them to consider whether or not they should be reviewed.[28] The Commissioner accepted this advice.[29] He felt entitled to inquire whether a department had reviewed a rule in the light of the hardship suffered by a complainant. But he stressed the point that it was a matter for the department to decide whether or not the rule should be altered; it was not a matter for him.[30]

From departmental rules, it was a short step to statutory orders. Here it was necessary to make a distinction between statutory orders which fell into the category of Statutory Instruments subject to review already by the Select Committee of the House of Commons on Statutory Instruments and those which were not. The former, as explained already, were scrutinised on a number of grounds and it was possible to draw the attention of the House of Commons to them. It would not be appropriate for the Commissioner or the Select Committee on the Parliamentary Commissioner to trespass in this field. But the select committee did recom-

[27] H.C. 334 of 1971–72, Qus. 102–109.
[28] H.C. 350 of 1967–68, pp. viii–ix.
[29] H.C. 9 of 1968–69.
[30] H.C. 129 of 1968–69, p. 6.

mend that " it would be proper for the Commissioner to investigate any complaint of maladministration in the administrative process leading to the making and subsequent reviewing of orders which are not Statutory Instruments." They recommended also that, in the case of Statutory Instruments themselves, while the Commissioner would not look at the making of the instruments, he would, in a case under investigation, inquire into the action taken by a department to review the operation of the instrument.[31] The Commissioner accepted this advice.[32]

It is proper to stress the restrictions upon the Commissioner's powers, both in respect of the channel through which complaints to him may come—the Member of Parliament—and the areas from which he is excluded, such as local government, the health service, the police, the nationalised industries and so on. At the same time it is proper also to stress that, granted that the Commissioner is operating within the area of his function, he is furnished with very strong inquisitorial powers. There is no restriction upon his power to obtain information (though there is on his power to make it public) nor upon the persons whom he may investigate. In particular he may question not only civil servants but Ministers also, and has already done so.[33] In this respect the British Parliamentary Commissioner has greater powers than the Commissioner in New Zealand who can investigate recommendations made to Ministers but cannot investigate the decisions of Ministers. It is to be noted that a Minister may not veto an investigation by the Commissioner. These are strong powers.

31 H.C. 385 of 1968–69, p. vii.
32 H.C. 138 of 1969–70. First Report of the Commissioner.
33 In the Duccio case, Stacey, *op. cit.*, pp. 310–311.

V

How effective has been their exercise? The detailed answer is found in the annual reports of the Commissioner which cannot be adequately summarised here. The short answer is that he has been remarkably effective. A less short answer may mention a few features of interest and importance. The first is that a very severe test of the Commissioner's effectiveness confronted him in his first year of office in what is called the Sachsenhausen case.[34] He survived the test with great distinction. A word or two of explanation is called for.[35] This was a complaint, forwarded to the Commissioner by Mr. Airey Neave M.P., that four people had been unjustly denied compensation by the Foreign Office under a scheme by which compensation was to be paid to British nationals or their dependants who had suffered loss of liberty, damage to their health, or death as a result of Nazi persecution. A sum of £1,000,000 had been paid by the West German Government to the United Kingdom Government for this purpose. The Foreign Office administered this scheme and laid down rules of eligibility by which applicants had to show either that they had been detained in a Nazi concentration camp or, if their place of detention was not a concentration camp, that the conditions they had experienced were comparable to those in a concentration camp.

The Foreign Office had decided that three of the complainants had not been held in a concentration camp but in adjoining areas which were not part of the camp proper, and that they had not endured conditions of severity com-

[34] H.C. 54 of 1967–68. Third Report of the Commissioner.
[35] It is well summarised in Stacey, *op. cit.*, pp. 248–258.

parable to those experienced in concentration camps. This decision was contested by the applicants. But in spite of pressure at every level in the ministerial hierarchy from 1965 the decision remained unchanged. The case was referred to the Commissioner on May 23, 1967, soon after he took office, and he proceeded personally to undertake a most detailed investigation. His conclusions were that (1) the process by which the Foreign Office decided that the applicants were not in the Sachsenhausen concentration camp proper was based on partial and largely irrelevant information, (2) that the rule under which the Foreign Office was working meant that a non-camp claimant had to pass a more severe test of eligibility than a camp claimant and that this actually happened in the case of Sachsenhausen, and (3) that the claimants had suffered injustice in that "the rejection of their claim, and the terms in which the rejection had been defended by the Foreign Office had done harm to their standing and reputation."

The Foreign Secretary, Mr. George Brown, decided to reverse his decision and to pay compensation to the claimants. He still did not accept the finding of the Parliamentary Commissioner that there had been maladministration by the Foreign Office, but he conceded that "having established the office of Parliamentary Commissioner, whether I think his judgment is right or wrong, I am certain that it would be wrong to reject his views."[36] And he accepted full individual ministerial responsibility.[37] It was an impressive demonstration of the value of the Parliamentary Commissioner and it established the reputation of the office at the outset. It gave scope also to the select

[36] H.C.Deb., Vol. 758, 5 s., col. 116.
[37] *Ibid.*, col. 112.

committee to pursue questions of the exercise of the Commissioner's powers and of the steps taken by departments to remedy maladministration when it had been identified.

A second feature of the record of the Commissioner's work is the variety of cases with which he has dealt. It is interesting to notice that he is able to investigate certain aspects of planning decisions, in spite of the fact that there is a procedure for an inquiry. He can consider whether in fact the procedure has been properly followed and whether there has been undue delay.[38] In cases where a tribunal is provided, there can be aspects of the matter which fall within the ambit of the Parliamentary Commissioner.[39] It is interesting to see how different institutions intended to prevent or remedy maladministration can co-operate in this way. Strictly speaking one might expect that a question arising out of what might be thought of as the inadequacy of a tribunal or inquiry to deal with maladministration would be a matter for the Council on Tribunals. But there is an overlap between the work of the Council and the work of the Parliamentary Commissioner and this was recognised right at the start by providing that the Parliamentary Commissioner should be *ex officio* a member of the Council. Experience so far suggests that the Commissioner has been more effective than the Council in dealing with some of the inadequacies that seem to have arisen from the working of the tribunals or inquiries. His direct and unimpeded access to the government departments and his link with the select committee give him an advantage over the Council.

So far as inquiries are concerned it is likely that a

38 There were three cases in the Annual Report for 1971. H.C. 116 of 1971–72, pp. 92 and 99.

39 H.C. 138 of 1969–70.

delay by the department in coming to decisions will be the commonest complaint by the citizen. Thus, in one of the cases in 1971 to which the Commissioner drew attention in his report, the Minister had dismissed an appeal against the recommendation of the inspector who had held the inquiry and the Commissioner found that the whole operation took sixty-five weeks in all as compared with an average of about forty-two weeks for cases which went to inquiry. Of course there is a problem here, as in most matters of administration, of balancing speed with fairness and justice. At the same time, as the select committee remarked, "to the applicant, undue delay both causes annoyance and can produce hardship." [40] What emerged, however, was that the department was short of inspectors—they needed another thirty, to add to the 200 in post, to deal with the number of appeals which had increased from 6,000 to 8,000 in the preceding year.[41]

So far as tribunals are concerned, if there is a direct complaint to the Commissioner about the way in which a tribunal has worked, he passes it to the Council on Tribunals and is able, as an *ex officio* member of the Council, to follow it through. Where he can intervene himself, however, is in a case, of which there was an example in his annual report of 1969, where he found that the information given by the Ministry of Social Security to the Pensions Appeal Tribunal was not entirely correct. The Commissioner came to the conclusion, after investigation, that there had been "no attempt, at any time, to prejudice the hearing

[40] H.C. 334 of 1971–72, p. xiv.

[41] In the Commissioner's Fourth Report for 1972–73, he severely criticised the procedure of the Department of the Environment, which, though there had been no actual change of circumstances, produced two contrary decisions by the department within a few months.

of the appeal by the deliberate withholding of information," [42] and he did not therefore make a finding of maladministration.

In the annual league table of complaints and of findings of maladministration the Inland Revenue, the Department of the Environment and the Department of Health and Social Security, are usually found at the top. This is not surprising, for, as the Commissioner said, in giving evidence to the select committee on March 1, 1972, " these three departments are the ones in which the civil servants are most frequently in direct contact with members of the public." [43] But he adds, " in all these cases the complaints which come to me are a tiny fraction of the number of transactions between these departments and members of the public." The Inland Revenue usually has topped the league table and the chairman of the board of Inland Revenue appears regularly before the select committee. He explains that the board has 25,000,000 customers, " unwilling customers " as he has called them, and that the number of complaints, in " proportion to the number of transactions is remarkably small." [44] In evidence to the select committee on April 12, 1972, he stressed the fact that constant criticism of the staff of the Inland Revenue Department was likely to lead to a lowering of morale with, as one result, the loss to the department of " quality-staff." [45]

In our first chapter we mentioned that maladministration might be expected from a department which dealt with taxation, not only because of the number of transactions involved, but more perhaps because of the complication and

[42] H.C. 138 of 1969–70, p. 32, paras. 12 and 13.
[43] H.C. 334 of 1971–72, Qu. 110.
[44] H.C. 334 of 1971–72, Qu. 223.
[45] *Ibid.*

detail necessarily involved in the subject matter of the department. And with frequent changes in tax law, to a large or small extent almost every year, a great burden is thrown upon the staff, who (the chairman said in 1972), in recent years, in large proportions, were still under training and "they obviously could not be knowledgeable."[46] All the explanations seem plausible. They justify the existence of the Parliamentary Commissioner, however, in taking up these cases. What is not always so satisfactory is the attitude taken by the Inland Revenue when the question of remedying an injustice is raised. A case in point was the absence of a financial remedy, such as the payment of interest, in cases of delay in the repayment of tax. This was discussed in the sessions of 1970–71 and in 1971–72, but objections were made by the board on grounds of impracticability and of increase of staff if the problem were to be treated comprehensively. The select committee in its report in 1972[47] could only say that while they recognised the practical problems "nevertheless they do not consider that where a taxpayer alleges undue delay by the department and this is clearly established, whether before or after the amount to be repaid is agreed, the case should remain unremedied. Your committee feel that in such cases it should be possible in the individual case to arrive at a commonsense judgment on the extent to which the department's own handling of the case has been unreasonably slow, and on the amount of interest justified to remedy the injustice caused by the period of the delay. It seems, to your committee, unreasonable for the Inland Revenue to withhold this remedy because of the practical problems of establishing in

[46] *Ibid.*, Qu. 224.
[47] *Ibid.*, p. xi, para. 24.

other cases whether there has been undue delay. They note that, by contrast, the taxpayer himself in certain circumstances is required to pay interest to the Inland Revenue on tax not paid within two months."

There is occasionally a "bureaucratic" (in the bad sense) element in the defence which departments make to the Commissioner's findings of maladministration and the Inland Revenue, it seems to me, errs in this way. There were traces of it also in the response made by the Department of Health and Social Security to a finding of the Commissioner that there had been a failure to give proper advice in a leaflet issued to persons approaching retirement age about the difference between tax free sickness benefit and taxable retirement pension, and that compensation should be paid to the complainant. The Department contended that there would be formidable administrative difficulties in identifying all those who might have been affected by the lack of information and that they would require acceptable medical evidence of qualification for sickness benefit and that this would be difficult to obtain. They also decided that they would not be justified in providing a remedy limited to those who took the initiative and claimed and who could produce reliable evidence of incapacity.[48] There was considerable discussion of this attitude in the select committee, and it was in the course of it that the exchange occurred between Dame Irene Ward and Dame Mildred Riddelsdell recorded in the last chapter. The select committee could do no more than "express their disappointment and regret that the Department were not prepared to give redress to people misled in that way and able to support

48 *Ibid.*, pp. xii and xiii, para. 30.

their claim with appropriate medical evidence." [49] And they were able also to reject the bureaucratic attitude sometimes advanced "that remedies should not be afforded, when an injustice has been brought to light by the Parliamentary Commissioner, on the grounds that this would be unfair to those who have not complained." [50] So does equity get in the way of justice.

VI

But the general verdict of the select committee is that "government departments are very ready to accept the views of the Parliamentary Commissioner and to afford a remedy for injustice." [51] The Commissioner works with a staff of about sixty. About half of them are engaged upon investigations on behalf of and under the instructions of the Commissioner combing departmental files and examining departmental officials. In an appropriate case (Sachsenhausen was an example) the Commissioner himself takes personal charge. The Commissioner has adopted the practice of sending his investigating officers to visit those who have complained (usually in their own homes) in cases when it seems that they might have relevant additional information to impart.[52] The staff embody their evidence in a report to the Commissioner and make their recommendations "on which I arrive at my personal conclusion as to the result of the investigation. This I embody in a results report which I render to the Member who referred the complaint to me, with a copy to the principal officer of the department. Before issuing

[49] *Ibid.*, para. 32.
[50] *Ibid.*, para. 33.
[51] *Ibid.*, para. 33.
[52] *Ibid.*, Qu. 101.

the report I check with the department the correctness and presentation of the facts concerning them as embodied in the report."[53] In this way we see the Parliamentary Commissioner, like the Comptroller and Auditor-General, penetrating, on behalf of Parliament, behind the veil which screens officials from their gaze and coming back in due course to report what he has found. The methods are, of necessity, slightly different. The Comptroller and Auditor-General's staff work in and upon the accounts of the department there continuously, as the nature of audit requires. The officials of the Parliamentary Commissioner go in when required as the result of a complaint. Though the reports of both tend to preserve the anonymity of the officials concerned, those of the Parliamentary Commissioner go even further by not disclosing the name of the Member of Parliament who forwarded the complaint or the name of the complainant.

The record of the Parliamentary Commissioner since the inception of the office in 1967 is, in my opinion, impressive. But, we must add immediately, he is good as far as he goes, or as far as he is allowed to go. For the remarkable thing about the office are the restrictions upon its powers. The Commissioner may only entertain a complaint if it is referred to him by a Member of Parliament. This restriction has led some students to say that it is incorrect to call the Commissioner an "Ombudsman." The restriction has been criticised from the outset as unwise or unnecessary. What effect it has on preventing complaints from reaching the Commissioner is difficult to discover, and what conclusions one could draw if we did know how many cases were blocked

[53] H.C. 134 of 1967–68, p. 6, para. 14.

in this way is a matter of conjecture. We must take into account the fact that there are other methods of dealing with complaints through the intervention of a Member of Parliament than referral to the Commissioner. In a recent study of this aspect of the Commissioner's work it is stated: "Members of Parliament do use the office very sparingly indeed by comparison with the frequency with which they employ the established techniques for helping constituents." [54] It is clear that in many cases a Member of Parliament can deal with a constituent's complaint more expeditiously by personal action than by making a reference to the Commissioner. The usual length of time taken by the Commissioner to deal with a case is from three to five months.[55] "In terms of rapid results, the office obviously cannot compete with alternative methods of redressing grievances." [56] ". . . if Members make use of the office relatively infrequently, it may be because, in their view, the alternative informal and parliamentary methods of helping constituents are more effective than the efforts of the Commissioner." [57] There has been a steady decline in the number of cases reaching the office over the past five years.[58] Yet are we to conclude that because of what is called "the M.P. filter," [59] the citizen has been denied opportunities to have his grievances redressed? Perhaps what we have—and it is what some people intended all along—is not so much a new and additional safeguard against the possibility of admini-

[54] Roy Gregory and Alan Alexander, "Our Parliamentary Ombudsman" (Pt. II) in (1973) 51 *Public Administration* 48.

[55] First Report of Select Committee, 1970–71.

[56] Roy Gregory and Alan Alexander, *loc. cit.*, p. 50.

[57] *Ibid.*, p. 51.

[58] *Ibid.*, p. 58.

[59] See Lionel H. Cohen, "The Parliamentary Commissioner and the 'M.P. Filter'" in [1972] P.L. 204.

strative injustice as a strengthening of the protection already offered by Members of Parliament.[60] And it is conceivable that out of this the citizen has gained, not lost.

But what can we conclude when we read that in 1971 out of the complaints actually referred to the Commissioner by Members of Parliament, complaints which have passed through the filter, about 50 per cent. are still rejected, because they were outside the Commissioner's terms of reference? [61] The greater part of them were rejected because the complaints were not against any of the government departments or bodies listed in Schedule 2 to the Act of 1967 or because they referred to personnel matters which are excluded by paragraph 10 of Schedule 3 to the Act. This whole subject of areas excluded from the Parliamentary Commissioner's investigation has been of lively interest to the select committee from the first year of its operation, when they reported in July 1968 that though they accepted that the police forces, both metropolitan and provincial, were outside the jurisdiction of the Commissioner, they were not satisfied that the hospital service was excluded from his jurisdiction.[62] Since that date, decisions have been taken which widen the area in which a procedure for the redress of grievances is to be made available to the citizen. In fact this may lead to a widening of the area in which the Parliamentary Commissioner himself will operate, but in some other matters new institutions will be established.

On February 22, 1972, the Secretary of State for Social Services announced in the House of Commons that it was the government's intention to establish a Health Service Com-

[60] Roy Gregory and Alan Alexander, *loc. cit.*, p. 42.
[61] H.C. 334 of 1971–72, Evidence of the Commissioner, p. 1, Qu. 101.
[62] H.C. 350 of 1967–68, pp. xiii–xiv.

missioner for England, one for Scotland and one for Wales; that it was contemplated that, for a start at any rate, the three posts should be held by one person; that the work of the Health Commissioner should be associated with that of the Parliamentary Commissioner, and that there were strong arguments for considering whether all the posts should not be held by the same person. In a sense it could be said that this was a proposal to extend the area of jurisdiction of the Parliamentary Commissioner to the health service. The Secretary of State indicated that he proposed to discuss the matter with the Select Committee on the Parliamentary Commissioner. The outcome of their discussions, at the moment of writing, appears to be that the Secretary of State contemplates one person holding all the appointments—a proposal which the select committee favoured—and that this person, at the outset at any rate, is to be the Parliamentary Commissioner for Administration. Thus there should exist broadly a similar relationship between the Health Commissioner and the select committee as existed with the Parliamentary Commissioner. It was contemplated also that complaints to the Health Commissioner might be forwarded through Members of Parliament but that they should not be the sole channel of approach.[63] In the outcome it appears that the Health Commissioner may be approached direct, but he must see first that the Health Authority has first been given the chance to investigate and reply to the complaint before the Commissioner himself begins his investigation.[64]

A decision of equal importance was announced by the Secretary of State for the Environment on November 16,

63 H.C. 72 of 1972–73. Annual Report of the Commissioner, p. 11.

64 See article by Lionel H. Cohen in *Public Administration,* Vol. 51, 1973: "Local Government Complaints: The M.P.'s viewpoint."

1971, during the debate on the second reading of the Local Government Bill in the House of Commons. He said that the government proposed to initiate the setting up of a complaints machinery for local government in England and Wales. In March 1972 the Secretary of State submitted a memorandum outlining the scheme to the Select Committee on the Parliamentary Commissioner and also appeared before them to give evidence. At the time of writing the final details are not known, and discussions about the appropriate machinery must of course be undertaken with the representatives of local authorities and their staff. The new system of local government does not come into operation until April 1974 and the local commissioners for administration would not begin their work until then. In the meantime it is of interest to mention in broad outline what was proposed.

The existing machinery for dealing with complaints in local government consists substantially in the right of the citizen to draw the attention of the clerk or other senior officer of a council to them or to report them to a councillor who will investigate and if necessary raise the matter in a committee or, in public, at a council meeting. These methods are by no means ineffective, but it can be seen that, to a large extent, the complaints will be investigated by those whose conduct or decision is itself complained of.[65] "The Government are of the opinion," said the Secretary of State in his memorandum, "that a citizen who believes himself to be the victim of maladministration by a local authority, should enjoy the same right to have his complaint independently scrutinised as he enjoys through the Parliamentary Commissioner for Administration in respect of

[65] H.C. 334 of 1971–72, pp. xv–xvi.

alleged maladministration by the central government. They envisage that this could be achieved by creating an independent statutory commission for local administration to deal with complaints of maladministration by local authorities. . . ."[66] The commission would consist of a number of local commissioners for administration (not less than nine probably), appointed by the Crown to ensure independence, each working independently in a particular area of the country. Complaints would normally be made to a councillor of the authority complained of and referred by him, but there should be a discretion in the commissioner to accept and investigate a complaint directly addressed to him, if he thought there were special circumstances which made it proper to do so.[67]

The Secretary of State regarded these proposals as essentially an adaptation of the system of the Parliamentary Commissioner for Administration to the different constitutional position of local government. "Just as the Parliamentary Commissioner for Administration was conceived primarily as assisting Members of Parliament to protect the rights and interests of individual constituents *vis-à-vis* central government, so the local commissioners are seen as assisting local councillors in protecting the rights and interests of their electors *vis-à-vis* the local authority."[68] And similar restrictions are proposed upon the powers of the local government commissioners as upon those of the Parliamentary Commissioner. They are to entertain only complaints alleging injustice as a consequence of maladministration, and this would not include cases where the complainant had been no

[66] H.C. 334 of 1971–72, p. 9; Secretary of State's Memorandum, para. 4.
[67] *Ibid.*, para. 5.
[68] *Ibid.*, para. 11.

differently affected by the action in question than the general body of ratepayers.[69] Nor could the commissioners investigate personnel matters, or contractual and other commercial transactions, or any action in respect of which the complainant had an alternative remedy, such as a right of appeal to a Minister or to the courts, to which he could reasonably be expected to resort.[70]

It may be worth recording, at this point, that the select committee has, on more than one occasion, expressed its view that the exclusion of personnel matters from the jurisdiction of the Parliamentary Commissioner is unwarranted and that the Act of 1967 should be amended to remove this restriction.[71] But the government has consistently rejected their suggestions.[72] They believe that the existing internal arrangements to deal with staff difficulties through the Whitley Council machinery are more appropriate. They maintain that the Parliamentary Commissioner Act was intended to deal with complaints by a citizen against the government, not by employees against their employer. So far it would seem that civil servants through their representative bodies, whatever view they may take of the existing machinery (and they will have more than one view), do not wish to replace it by the Parliamentary Commissioner.[73]

In one other area of importance also, proposals have been envisaged for an improvement in the procedure for dealing with complaints, namely, the police. Here, as mentioned already, the Parliamentary Commissioner has no

[69] *Ibid.*, para. 9.
[70] *Ibid.*, para. 8.
[71] H.C. 334 of 1971–72; Second Report of the Select Committee. The restriction is found in Sched. 3, para. 10, to the Act.
[72] Cmnd. 4661.
[73] According to Sir William Armstrong: H.C. 285 of 1968–69, p. 128, question 523.

jurisdiction. There is a good deal of criticism of the existing methods. The Home Secretary, in a debate in the House of Commons on a private member's Bill in 1973,[74] gave a general indication that some proposals might be forthcoming. It is clearly a most serious gap in the machinery for dealing with complaints by the citizen, yet the difficulties in the way of devising a procedure which can do justice to all the parties concerned are enormous.

74 H.C.Deb., Vol. 851, 5 s., cols. 934 *et seq.* He spoke of introducing an independent element on Ombudsman lines into the process of inquiry: col. 993.

CHAPTER 6

APPRAISAL

I

PERHAPS the most striking feature in the search for more effective remedies for maladministration in the last twenty years has been the discovery of the Ombudsman or his equivalent. An institution which was long established in Sweden, and adopted more recently in the other Scandinavian countries in various forms, has now become of interest to many other countries [1] and in some significant cases has been imported, usually in some adapted or naturalised form, and established as part of the machinery for the prevention and remedy of maladministration. The examples of New Zealand and Britain are of particular interest to us.[2] But

[1] See, *e.g.* Walter Gellhorn, *When Americans Complain* (Harvard U.P., 1966) and *Ombudsman and Others: Citizens Protectors in Nine Countries*; and Stanley V. Anderson (ed.) *Ombudsman for American Government* (American Assembly, 1968).

[2] It is worth recalling that a Parliamentary Commissioner for Northern Ireland was established in Northern Ireland by the Stormont Legislature in 1969 and that Sir Edmund Compton was invited to accept the office. In December 1969 the Stormont Government appointed also a Commissioner for Complaints to investigate complaints against local authorities and other public bodies, including hospitals and health authorities, but excluding those departments which were under the jurisdiction of the Parliamentary Commissioner for Northern Ireland. Complaints to the Parliamentary Commissioner had to be forwarded through a Member of the Stormont Parliament, those to the Commissioner for Complaints were to be sent direct. See article by H. J. Elcock, "Opportunity for Ombudsman" in (1972) 50 *Public Administration.*

perhaps the most surprising news of all was conveyed to readers of *The Times* on January 26, 1973, when its Paris correspondent, Charles Hargrove, reported as follows:

> "Everyone in France, from President Pompidou downwards, readily acknowledges that one of the plagues from which the country suffers is an over-centralised, inhuman and bureaucratic administration. It treats the citizen as if he were at its service instead of the other way round and overwhelms him with a mass of regulations, circulars and forms.
>
> "To attempt to remedy this situation, M. Michael Poniatowski, Secretary-General of the Independent Republican Party, suggested a couple of years ago the creation of a French Ombudsman, who would cut administrative corners and redress the abuses and wrongs of bureaucracy. After much hesitation and discussion, the Government took up the proposal, although in diluted form. It was agreed by Parliament last December and became law three weeks ago. Now the Government has announced that M. Antoine Pinay, the former Prime Minister, will be the first to hold this perilous post, at the age of eighty-one."

He holds the post of *Médiateur* or Mediator, the term in France for Ombudsman.

To those who believed—and there have appeared to be some—that the citizen in France enjoyed, through the *Conseil d'Etat*, all the protection that he or anyone else could require from maladministration, the need for an Ombudsman must have come as a surprise, and that such an office should be established a greater surprise still. But greatest surprise of all must have been to many that a former politician of eighty-one should be chosen to fill the post. It seems obvious that there is a great deal still to be discovered before we can form any reliable idea of what the office of *Médiateur* in France is expected to do, how it is expected to work, and what effect it will have.[3]

The advantages of such an office as Ombudsman in any country may be readily appreciated. From the citizen's point of view the procedure is simple and cheap. It resembles, in some sense, an opportunity to consult a lawyer without fear or obligation. The mass of citizens in Britain dread entanglement with lawyers and particularly because of expense. To send a complaint to an Ombudsman, whether through a Member of Parliament or not, means that someone with skill, whose job it is, will investigate all the complicated parts of your case and tell you where you stand. It is true that he may have to tell you that you have a grievance but that you have also a legal remedy and that you must use it, if you seek redress. But you will have discovered that much at least, free of charge and with no obligation. You will not have got yourself into the hands of the lawyers. It is interesting that the word "Ombudsman" means attorney or legal representative in Swedish; he is the citizens' attorney. There is a sense in which this function is an important part

[3] Loi no° 73–6 du Janvier 3, 1973 instituant un mediateur. He is appointed for six years, not renewable, by decree of the Council of Ministers. He appears to have jurisdiction throughout the public service. There are resemblances to the British Parliamentary Commissioner in the duties of the post. Complaints must be forwarded through a deputy or a senator, and they transmit them if they think they fall within his competence and deserve his attention (Art. 6). He has access to all documents and must be given all assistance (except in such matters as national defence) by Ministers and all other officials (Arts. 12 and 13). He reports to the President and to Parliament (Art. 14). He is given immunity in respect of words said or acts done in the exercise of his functions (Art. 3).

of his services. But in Britain, of course, the Parliamentary Commissioner and the proposed commissioners in local government and the health services are normally debarred from dealing with cases where the complainant has an alternative remedy such as an appeal to a Minister or to the courts. They have a discretion to take up such cases if they think it unreasonable to require the complainant to use this remedy. It is necessary to record, therefore, that although the Ombudsman performs in some measure the function of the citizens' attorney, there is a limit to the help he can give. In a whole range of complaints, resort to tribunals and to courts is required, with the attendant advantages and disadvantages, financially and procedurally, which such recourse involves, as was explained in Chapter 2. This must be weighed up in our appraisal in due course.

But the striking advantage of the Ombudsman is that he can go behind the screen and investigate fully all that has happened in the case, and that he does this as an independent and skilled authority. This is something which the Member of Parliament cannot do because he would be interfering with the autonomous executive and in Britain there is no area where the doctrine of the separation of powers is so strictly enforced as in the area of executive and administrative functions, whatever the textbooks may say about Cabinet government and the parliamentary executive. The Minister, of course, has full authority to investigate and that is one of the things individual responsibility includes. But in practice he cannot. He must rely on his officials to do it for him. Therefore the Ombudsman and his staff are authorised to investigate and it is no exaggeration to say that the Parliamentary Commissioner Act of 1967 did authorise an encroachment on the doctrine of ministerial responsibility.

". . . Parliament has undermined the doctrine to some extent, in that the power of the Commissioner to carry out an independent investigation within the department and publish what he finds, is an encroachment upon the Minister's responsibility." [4]

The authority to go behind the veil is a power which the Parliamentary Commissioner shares with a tribunal of inquiry set up under the Act of 1921, but, as was explained in Chapter 4, these tribunals are exceptional, whereas the work of the Commissioner is usual and routine. Both are encroachments upon the responsibility of Ministers. But they exhibit one difference which has led to discussion of some importance in connection with remedies for maladministration. Tribunals usually sit in public; the Commissioner conducts all his inquiries in private. In a number of cases where tribunals of inquiry have sat and reported civil servants have been named and blamed in public, whereas the reports of the Commissioner are as thoroughly "anonymised" (to use his expression) as possible. It is interesting to recall that, in the case of the collapse of the Vehicle and General Insurance Company, the Parliamentary Commissioner had already begun an investigation before the tribunal had been appointed, and abandoned his inquiry when the tribunal was established. It is tempting to speculate what the outcome of the Commissioner's investigation might have been, and whether the names of any civil servants would have been mentioned either in the report of the Commissioner or in any discussion of it in the Select Committee on the Parliamentary Commissioner.[5]

4 H.C. 350 of 1967–68, p. xi.

5 It is interesting to compare the Commissioner's investigation of the conduct of the Department of Trade and Industry in relation to

The controversy that arose in 1968 about calling a particular civil servant from the Foreign Office before the Select Committee on the Parliamentary Commissioner has already been discussed in Chapter 4. It is clearly the view of the government that the select committee shall follow the practice of the Public Accounts Committee and deal only with the principal officers of a department who could speak collectively on its behalf. There is a difficult issue here. The Attorney-General argued forcefully for the view, in words that have been quoted already, that " the action of the department is action for which the department is collectively responsible and for which the Minister in charge is alone answerable to Parliament . . . I submit it is a corollary of the principle that it is the Minister alone who is responsible for the actions of his department that the individual civil servant who has contributed to the collective decision of the department should remain anonymous." [6]

Part of the case against this view was expressed in a paragraph which failed to become incorporated in the report of the select committee on this issue but which is recorded in the proceedings. It puts the point well. Mr. Alexander Lyon M.P., a member of the select committee, moved it and it runs as follows [7]:

> " There is no necessary correlation between the fact that a minister is answerable to Parliament for the workings of his department and the fiction that the department is collectively responsible for all decisions of the department. It is right that the House should have the power to discuss

certain insurance companies and his criticisms of its performance, which is found in the Fourth Report of the Commissioner for 1972–73.

6 H.C. 350 of 1967–68, p. 73.

7 *Ibid.*, p. xix.

the deficiencies of a government department but it is important to remember the practical limitations. Most acts of maladministration are not sufficiently grave to raise on the floor of the House and certainly do not merit or receive attention in a full debate. Whenever a controversial example of defective administration is fully debated, the issues are clouded by inadequate information available to members and the acrimony which may develop between the political parties. The result is influenced more by the Whips than by the effectiveness of the criticism. It would be more sensible to discuss individual acts of maladministration in the detached atmosphere of a select committee so that criticism could be accurate and informed. Debates in the House could then concentrate on the real issues. The result of this procedure would be that responsibility would fasten upon those who had actually committed an act of maladministration, whether civil servant or Minister, but, in the view of your committee, this would lead to an improvement in administration."

The position seems to be this. The Parliamentary Commissioner conducts his investigations in private. He has the power however to identify individual civil servants involved in the matters he is investigating. The Attorney-General conceded that this was so.[8] A complaint might be directed against a specific official, for example. There is provision also in the Parliamentary Commissioner Act for certain safeguards for civil servants who might find themselves becoming individually implicated in an investigation.[9] It is thus envisaged that in certain circumstances a report from the

[8] *Ibid.*, p. 73, col. 1.
[9] s. 7 (1) and (2).

Commissioner could infringe the anonymity of the individual civil servant.[10] There remains the question whether, if he has not so named an official, the select committee should regard it as appropriate to call such an official as a witness to inform themselves, for example, about the nature of the defect in the system which led to the acts of maladministration and about the measures taken to remedy the defect or for other purposes to obtain evidence from subordinate officials who are concerned at first hand with the actions in question. On this point the select committee recorded that, on infrequent occasions, such action might be necessary and they would feel capable of doing so without exposing officials to unfair publicity or criticism.[11]

It seems to me that these provisions for the naming of individual civil servants by the Commissioner, in exceptional cases (which the Act clearly authorises), and the assertion by the select committee that it reserves the right to summon an individual civil servant in certain (admittedly infrequent and exceptional) cases, add up to a safeguard against the abuse of the anonymity of civil servants which is substantial. To ask for more seems to me to overlook and underestimate the effectiveness of the Commissioner's investigation. It is in private, but it is of course known in the department that an investigation is being carried out. It is known to the principal officer of the department for the complaint is referred to him at the outset. A circle of officials, including the superiors and colleagues of any officials who are clearly involved in the investigation, will know what is going on and what the outcome of the investigation is. These are effective sanctions against maladministration; they involve professional reputa-

10 H.C. 350 of 1967–68, p. xi.
11 *Ibid.*, p. xii, para. 30.

tions, both of individuals, divisions of a department or the department as a whole.

II

Of course our belief in the effectiveness of this method of remedying maladministration is founded in the end on the capacity and integrity of the Parliamentary Commissioner himself. His judgment of when it is proper to name an official, and our faith in his refusal to "cover up" for a department are the foundations upon which the whole system works. And as more areas are opened up to the investigation of Commissioners—in the health service, in local government and the police—the tests of the effectiveness of the system will be more severe, particularly when it comes to remedying the acts of maladministration. For, in Britain, the whole system as it exists at present is based upon the understanding that it is not the Commissioner who rights the wrongs, but the government. The Commissioner advises; if the government refuses to accept the advice, there is no more that the Commissioner can do, except to report it to the select committee and to Parliament. When we contemplate the extension of the Ombudsman system to, say, local government, can we expect wrongs to be righted with the same effectiveness as has, in general, been the experience of the Parliamentary Commissioner in dealing with British central government? [12] There are a number of questions here which deserve consideration.

The first is that the Parliamentary Commissioner has no power of his own motion to annul or amend or replace a decision which has been taken by a department, however

[12] Stacey, *op. cit.*, pp. 324–326.

much he may disapprove of it. He can report his opinion. He can advise, but no more. In this respect he resembles the Ombudsman of Scandinavia concerning whom Professor Herlitz says [13]: " As to the forms which the interventions of the Ombudsmen take when they find that something was wrong, it is worth emphasising that under no conditions are they empowered to quash decisions they disapprove of or to give orders to authorities or employees concerning the exercise of their administrative functions. The interventions of the Ombudsmen have, legally, nothing in common with the remedies afforded by superior authorities, courts and tribunals against wrong steps taken in administration." Yet in spite of this, " from the view points of citizens," continues Professor Herlitz, " the complaints to the Ombudsmen are easily understood as a sort of legal remedy." [14] And when we remember also that, as a matter of law, the *Conseil d'Etat* itself has " no effective means of enforcing compliance against an administration which is determined not to give way," [15] yet in practice it seldom fails to comply, we can understand that, in such circumstances, an opinion is in itself a decision. The Parliamentary Commissioner, so far, is in the position that a failure to comply with his recommendations is very rare, so that in this respect and to this extent, he compares well with Ombudsmen.

But although Ombudsmen have powers to advise and not to decide, they have in two cases, Sweden and Finland, a power to act as public prosecutors, suing the public employees in the general courts and demanding punishment (usually not very heavy) and sometimes damages.[16] Swedish

[13] *Element of Nordic Public Law*, pp. 192–193.
[14] *Ibid.*, p. 195.
[15] Brown and Garner, *French Administrative Law*, p. 137.
[16] Herlitz, *op. cit.*, p. 193.

and Finnish employees are subject to a comprehensive criminal responsibility. But it would appear that resort to prosecution has become rare in both countries.[17] In Denmark and Norway prosecution by the Ombudsmen is regarded as exceptional, and in New Zealand and Britain no such power is vested in him.[18] "In Denmark and Norway the essential form of intervening has, from the beginning, been the same: the Ombudsman has only to 'express his opinion.'"[19] So far this is the position in New Zealand and Britain.[20]

But the question is: "Upon what is he entitled to express his opinion?" and it is here that the restrictions upon the British Parliamentary Commissioner are noticeable, in comparison with the officers in Scandinavia or New Zealand or, in law at any rate, in France. We have said something of the restrictions upon the range of subjects which are excluded from his jurisdiction, although it is proposed now to widen this area in some measure, and of the restriction by the parliamentary "filter" (shared with the French "*Médiateur*"). Quite apart from these restrictions, however, there has been a good deal of misgiving expressed about the provision in section 12 (3) of the Act of 1967 where "it is hereby declared that nothing in this Act authorises or requires the Commissioner to question the merits of a decision taken without maladministration by a government department or other authority in the exercise of a discretion vested in that

[17] *Ibid.*, p. 193.

[18] But in Northern Ireland complainants may seek redress in the courts on the basis of a finding of maladministration by the Commissioner for Complaints. No case had been brought up to 1972. Elcock, *loc. cit.*, p. 90.

[19] Herlitz, *op. cit.*

[20] The first case in which a department declined to act in accordance with the Commissioner's recommendation seems to have occurred in 1970 and concerned the refusal of the Inland Revenue to repay a post-war credit. See Annual Report for 1970, H.C. 261, p. 139 (case C.565/L).

department or authority." The object of this provision, it was suggested, was to declare that it was not the function of the Commissioner to substitute his decision for that of the government.[21] The first Commissioner, Sir Edmund Compton, said in 1971 that " the job of the Commissioner is to review the administration of government and whilst I may question decisions taken with an element of maladministration, it is not for me to substitute my decision for the government decision." [22] In the area of maladministration attendant on discretionary decisions, the Commissioner thought that he could record as fact where a decision taken without maladministration nonetheless inflicted hardship on the complainant, but that, as regards the finding of maladministration his practice was to investigate the administrative processes attendant on the discretionary decision, but not to question the quality of the decision if he found no defect in the quality of the procedures.[23] Here, right at the outset of the British Commissioner's term of office, the Select Committee on the Commissioner took a vigorous initiative and urged him to strike out more boldly. They said that they felt " that the instances of maladministration found by the Commissioner might have been more in number and less trivial in content if he had allowed himself to find on occasion that a decision had been taken with maladministration because it was a bad decision." [24] This notion of the " bad decision," from the quality of which it would be proper to infer that there had been an element of maladministration in the making of it, was an important step towards making the Commissioner more effective. He agreed to follow the select committee's

[21] H.C. 350 of 1967–68, p. viii.
[22] H.C. 513 of 1970–71, p. 10.
[23] H.C. 354 of 1967–68, p. vii.
[24] *Ibid.*, p. iii.

suggestion, though he and they felt that the cases in which it arose would be rare.

There were, in fact, what looked like three cases of " bad decisions " in the Commissioner's Annual Report for 1970, and Mr. Geoffrey Marshall has analysed their significance in an illuminating article.[25] In one of the cases, the first case indeed where the Commissioner had questioned " a decision which was taken after proper consideration but [which] nevertheless was in his view bad in quality and ought to be reviewed," [26] was described by the Commissioner as a decision " taken on grounds which do not stand up to examination." [27] Here it was interesting to find that a member of the Select Committee in 1971 seemed to have forgotten the encouragement given by the committee in 1968, for he exclaimed, with truth but with surprise: " This is the first case, at least in my recollection, where a department's decision has been criticised not on grounds of delay, maladministration or anything of that sort but simply because the Commissioner thought that it was a wrong decision." And he described it as " a revolutionary thing to do." [28]

Although these examples of the application of the notion of the " bad " decision are rare, and reports from the Commissioner are often found in the form: " The decision was taken without maladministration; consequently I do not question the merits of the decision," it is interesting to ask what significance the finding of a " bad " decision amounts to, when it happens, particularly in relation to the Commissioner's assertion that it is not for him to substitute his decisions for those of the government. Mr. Marshall suggests that, while

[25] " Maladministration " [1973] P.L. 32.
[26] H.C. 513 of 1970–71, p. 34.
[27] H.C. 261 of 1970, p. 39.
[28] H.C. 513 of 1970–71, p. 34.

it is clear that the Parliamentary Commissioner, like other Ombudsmen, has no actual power to substitute his judgment for the government's in the sense of giving effect to a contrary decision, or indeed stating what would be the correct decision rather than stating that a wrong decision should be reconsidered, he can, in the course of reviewing a decision, disregard or contradict the judgment of the administrator, and in that sense substitute his own judgment to some degree. "To say that a decision has been wrongly or negligently reached or that it rests on irrelevant facts, wrongly balanced considerations, faulty logic or insubstantial evidence is to substitute the judgment that such is the case for the administrators' judgment that such is not the case." [29] It is a modest step, and understandably so in view of the wording of the Act in 1967; it is asking a lot, perhaps too much, of the British Commissioner to expect him to behave as if he were the New Zealand Commissioner, authorised under his Act of 1962, to report on decisions which are "unreasonable," "unjust," "oppressive" and "wrong." Mr. Marshall remarks on the restrictive effect which the use of the word "maladministration" has imported into the work of the Commissioner in Britain and wonders whether the time has not come to abandon the concept. I would suggest that we must construe the concept more widely, if we are to give it a meaning which is more in contact with administrative reality and less artificial.

III

The more we give our minds to devising methods of preventing or remedying maladministration, the more must we

[29] [1973] P.L., *ibid.*, pp. 35–36.

consider the balance between getting administration done justly and getting it done at all. The various devices to prevent maladministration tend to slow up the process of decision. As Sir William Armstrong said, in discussing with the Select Committee on the Parliamentary Commissioner in 1968 the effect of the setting up of the office upon government departments, there is the "dilemma between the need for speed on the one hand and the need for making sure you have all the facts on the other . . . That dilemma is there constantly. It can easily lead to rigidity: you have to have clear rules and so you get people to the point where they will just stick absolutely to the rules and even when a case turns up that is absurd, they will stick to them . . . . That meticulousness is there. It is, as some people would say, the vice of our civil service."[30] Every effort made to devise procedures to be followed in inquiries, for example, or in consultations is bound to slow up the process. Officials are aware that they act under the shadow of the parliamentary question or the scrutiny of the Select Committee or of action in the courts or of inquiry by the Parliamentary Commissioner, and all these influences work in the direction of meticulousness.

The setting up of the office of Parliamentary Commissioner raised fears that still more caution might be instilled in the civil servants, but it was the view of Sir William Armstrong that it might make little difference in practice in this respect, since all the other safeguards worked in the same direction. It is admitted, of course, that the Commissioner's inquiries are bound to take up time in the departments, and some departments suffer from this more than others because, *e.g.* the Inland Revenue, or Health and Social Security, or

[30] H.C. 350 of 1967–68, p. 109.

Environment have many dealings with the public. The Select Committee on the Parliamentary Commissioner has made a practice of asking officials from departments whether an undue burden is being placed upon their work through the existence of the Commissioner, or whether work is being slowed up or officials are becoming less inclined to take responsibility.[31] In most cases, heads of departments asserted that, though a price had to be paid in terms of time taken on Parliamentary Commissioner investigations, it was not an undue or significant burden, nor was the price unbearable or unfair but one which was right in the public interest.[32] And the Select Committee was gratified to find that the benefits derived from the office of Parliamentary Commissioner were still being achieved without any undue additional burden on the departments and without any significant slowing up of the work.

In judging these matters a great deal depends upon one's attitude to the exercise of power by officials. There are those who believe, to put it in an extreme form, that the less power officials exercise, the better; there are others who say that power must be conferred upon officials, and it is foolish to make it difficult or impossible for them to exercise it effectively. This difference of opinion or perhaps more accurately this difference of temperament, is sometimes detected in judges. We have judges described as " administration minded," which seems to mean that, if asked to construe a grant of power to officials, their attitude is to try and make sense of the grant, to make it work, to facilitate action by the official. Judges of a contrary temperament will wish to hedge the grant of

[31] *e.g.* in Second Report of 1967–68, H.C. 350, and in Second Report of 1971–72, H.C. 334.

[32] *e.g.* Principal officer of the Department of the Environment, H.C. 334 of 1971–72, p. viii.

power about with restrictions, which make action difficult and slow down administration almost to a halt. It is as a result of experiences of this kind that officials seek to insert into legislation granting power to them some provisions that prevent recourse to the courts. Yet which attitude, in the extreme form, does more to produce maladministration? Does the exercise of power by officials, riding rough shod over the citizens' objections, or does the spectacle of the administration grinding to a halt?

We do not need to deal in extremes, of course, but we are likely to have a temperamental preference for one side or the other. For the officials themselves, it is likely that they will be in an uncomfortable position because they will be criticised at one and the same time for delay and for riding rough shod. They will be urged to get something done; to cut the corners and the red tape; and at the same time to behave with equity, fairness, openness, and impartiality, all of which must result in delay.

While officials in Britain have testified that the setting up of the office of Parliamentary Commissioner, though causing them extra work, is justified and even welcome in the cause of good administration, they expressed from the outset a fear—transmitted to the select committee through the Head of the Home Civil Service—lest the investigation carried out in private by the Commissioner may be followed by a public re-investigation by the select committee.[33] This fear was expressed particularly at the time of the Sachsenhausen case when the select committee contemplated examining a particular official. What should our attitude be to this claim to anonymity by officials? In my opinion it should be in the most exceptional case only that the conduct of a named civil

[33] H.C. 350 of 1967–68, pp. 98–99.

servant should be investigated and reported upon publicly. There *could* be such cases, either in the proceedings of a select committee, whether that on public accounts or on expenditure or on the Parliamentary Commissioner; or it could occur in a tribunal of inquiry set up under the Act of 1921 or by a departmental Minister. But as a rule, it seems to me, on experience so far, the investigation of the Parliamentary Commissioner has important advantages which on balance make it preferable to the public investigation. It is true that the Commissioner's investigation is in private, and indeed the Act requires it. There are adequate safeguards for any official whose individual conduct comes under scrutiny: they are accepted by officials as fair.[34] The powers of the Commissioner to investigate are extensive, as has been explained already. His reports name the department, though not individual officials. His recommendations are known, and what action, if any, the department has taken is also known. This seems to me to provide a thorough and searching inquiry conducted with proper safeguards for those being inquired into and at the same time an element of publicity which no department could disregard or feel indifferent to, whether it was favourable or unfavourable.

The alternative of publicity has many serious drawbacks. It is easy to say that particular officials should be named. In very many cases it would not be practicable or just to do so—there are too many people involved with some sort of share of responsibility. Moreover it is doing to the employees in government departments something which is not done to the employees of other undertakings which have dealings with the public—banks, insurance companies, chain stores, suppliers of goods and services. These undertakings, indeed, are not

[34] *Ibid.*, p. 99.

subject even to investigation to the extent of that which government departments undergo at the hand of the Parliamentary Commissioner. To impose on public officials this more extreme criticism to which publicity would give rise seems to me to place them at a disadvantage which is not justifiable. But, it may be said, they are servants of the public, they must put up with " public criticism "; they are in a different position from employees of private concerns. Perhaps it is time that employees of private concerns were brought under stricter control, and their acts of maladministration investigated and reported upon, for they all should be serving the public. It seems to me that, so far as public officials are concerned, the result of wide-spread public criticism of named officials could be to cause a loss of morale and efficiency in the service, and a reluctance of able people to enter the service. If we require candidates of high quality in the service of the government, we cannot expect them to accept controls which discourage initiative or the taking of responsibility. All the traditional vices of the civil service would flourish under such a system—caution, passing the buck, delay. What the Parliamentary Commissioner can do in private investigation and by his published, " anonymised " reports, and what we may expect him to be able to do in the new areas of the health service and local government is considerable. If it is not enough, the direction in which his powers should be strengthened would seem to me to lie more effectively, not in the removal in some degree of the anonymity of the official, but in the removal still further of restrictions upon the matters which the Parliamentary Commissioner or other new commissioners may deal with, and of the barriers at present preventing direct access to them by members of the public through some form of " filter."

IV

There is one class of complaints which is, as a rule, intended to be excluded from the investigation of the Parliamentary Commissioner, and about which a little should be said. In the Act of 1967 the Commissioner is given a discretion whether or not to investigate cases where the complainant has or had a right of appeal to a tribunal or a remedy by way of proceedings in a court of law.[35] In the ordinary way the Commissioner will not deal with these complaints, nor does it seem to me that he should. But if we say this, we have to ask ourselves how satisfied we are with the remedies offered to the citizen who claims to have suffered from maladministration, who resorts to tribunals and courts. In Chapter 2 we have set out our main conclusions on this topic. There are clearly some causes for disquiet. The procedure through which resort to the courts may be undertaken as a remedy for maladministration is obviously in need of reform. Everybody who knows anything about the subject agrees that this is so. So long as the position is left as it is, we must acknowledge that a gap exists in the machinery for ensuring a remedy for maladministration.

But we must acknowledge also that even if the law were reformed, access to it must not be assumed to be effective or available to all. The law is expensive and most people are afraid to get entangled with it. While we must welcome the important steps recently taken with the passing of the Legal Advice and Assistance Act 1972 and the making of the Legal Advice and Assistance Regulations 1973, and the initiative of the Lord Chancellor's Legal Aid Advisory Committee in circulating, on June 27, 1973, a working paper

[35] s. 5 (2).

on legal aid in proceedings before tribunals, we will know that it will be a long time before resort to the courts for the remedying of maladministration will be as simple and cheap and expeditious as resort to the Parliamentary Commissioner in Britain or, as we are assured, resort to the *Tribunaux Administratifs* and the *Conseil d'Etat* is in France. Those of us who read the *Bulletin* of the Legal Action Group will be aware at one and the same time of the need for legal services to be made more readily available to citizens, of the encouraging development of legal advice centres in many parts of the country, and of the practical constraints " which will or may operate to prevent the new scheme of legal advice and assistance under the Act of 1972 from bringing lawyers' skills to bear in the areas of law which affect poor people." In a recent leading article in the *Bulletin*, the author mentions three constraints: the first is solicitors' unfamiliarity with these areas of law and, consequently, their understandable reluctance to enter into them. The second constraint is that solicitors are already over-burdened with work and therefore have no incentive to take on more and unfamiliar work. The third constraint on imaginative use of the new scheme could be the level of remuneration offered to solicitors under the scheme. A fourth, in the opinion of the writer of the article is that the Legal Aid area secretaries may not interpret the term " application of English law to any particular circumstances which have arisen in relation to the person seeking advice " (which occurs in section 2 (1) (*a*) of the Act of 1972) as broadly as it should be interpreted.[36] And there are insistent questions from time to time about whether the legal profession, organised as it is at present and with its present methods of recruitment, is likely to be able to recruit

[36] L. A. G. Bulletin, May 1973, p. 83.

enough lawyers for the work that must be undertaken if the Act of 1972 is to be operated effectively.

Here there is a gap in the arrangements in Britain for the remedying of maladministration through resort to the courts. But it is worthwhile to put it into some sort of perspective before we leap to the conclusion that Britain today still stands in insular exclusion from any effective control over administration by the use of the law, through the courts. Forty years ago the criticisms made of uncontrolled administrators, in books like Lord Hewart's *The New Despotism* and C. K. Allen's *Bureaucracy Triumphant* were concerned very much with the growth of tribunals, unknown to or outside of the ordinary courts of law, which were thought of as irregular and almost illegal. At the same time there were others, such as W. A. Robson who in *Justice and Administrative Law* welcomed these new developments but argued that they should be regularised and systematised so that Britain might obtain the best of the world of *droit administratif* without losing the virtues of its own legal system. In the years that have elapsed some changes have been made, although " the system," of which Professor Wade speaks, is still lacking and this, in his mind, is a serious defect in the British arrangements.

It is worth noting briefly some of the changes that have been made since, say, the publication of the Report of the Committee on Ministers' Powers in 1932.[37] The report led to no immediate action. Writers like C. K. Allen and W. A. Robson battled on in their advocacy of means to control the exercise of official power. With the end of the war things began to move. In the field of delegated legislation, with

[37] Cmd. 4060. (The Donoughmore-Scott Report, so named after its two chairmen.)

which half of the Report of the Committee on Ministers' Powers was concerned, the House of Commons in 1944, while the war was still on, established its Select Committee on Statutory Rules and Orders (later renamed the Select Committee on Statutory Instruments), and in 1946 Parliament passed the Statutory Instruments Act,[38] which came into effect on January 1, 1948. In the area of suits against the government, there was passed in 1947 the Crown Proceedings Act [39] which removed the immunity of the Crown from suit, a reform long advocated and long overdue. In the area of tribunals and inquiries the report of the Franks Committee of 1957 led to the Tribunals and Inquiries Act of 1958 [40] and the setting up of the Council on Tribunals, and in 1967 there came the Parliamentary Commissioner Act [41] and the inauguration of the British Ombudsman. And, finally, there has been the great change of mood in the courts in the exercise of judicial review which is described by Schwartz and Wade in vivid terms.[42] " The period of the forties and fifties," they say, " might be called ' the great depression ' . . . The result was that administrative law was at its lowest ebb for perhaps a century . . . All this now seems like a looking-glass world. Natural justice is being applied more widely and is producing more case law than ever before, and is providing a broad foundation for administrative due process . . . As for controlling the executive generally, the courts are probably more active in this respect than at any previous time, and they have fully shaken off their timidity." It is an impressive picture, but it cannot be left without mentioning once more

38 9 & 10 Geo. 6, c. 36.
39 10 & 11 Geo. 6, c. 44.
40 6 & 7 Eliz. 2, c. 68.
41 1967, c. 13.
42 *Legal Control of Government*, pp. 319–323.

(as Schwartz and Wade themselves are at pains to do) that " litigation in the High Court is formal and expensive, and it is unfortunate that the protection of the law is not cheap." [43]

V

We come back again to the Ombudsman who " takes up citizens' grievances at exactly the point where the law leaves off." [44] May I make three points about the office?

The first concerns what is sometimes called the " myth " or the " fiction " of individual ministerial responsibility. I do not quarrel with these terms, provided it is remembered that myths or fictions can often express an important truth in constitutional affairs. It seems to me that the fiction of individual ministerial responsibility ought not to be discarded, but equally that it ought not to be seen to be so completely remote from reality as to be partially misleading. The office of Parliamentary Commissioner for Administration or Ombudsman in Britain seems to me to provide a much needed support for individual ministerial responsibility. Far from weakening it, the office strengthens it. And it strengthens also the whole process of control within a department which, it would seem to me, should be welcomed by heads of departments and higher officials in a department, not resented. It gives some reality, some stuffing to the vague, elusive notion of the single responsible minister. In an unexpected way, perhaps, the introduction of the Ombudsman and the extension of the areas in which some such official is to operate, ensures a future for ministerial responsibility, in the relatively minor matters of maladministration in which its effectiveness in providing remedies is open to question or scepticism.

43 *Op. cit.*, p. 325.
44 *Ibid.*, p. 324.

Mention of the plans to extend the scope of an Ombudsman's activity in Britain leads to my second point. It is difficult to know how this widening of scope will affect the reputation of the office and its effectiveness. In an article published in *Public Law* in 1960, Mr. Louis Blom-Cooper feared "... a proliferation of regional Ombudsmen which would run the serious risk of depersonalising the institution. The Ombudsman must be a known man of absolute integrity in the eyes of the public and the civil service. If he ever became a department, the value of the institution would disappear. A bureaucracy upon a bureaucracy spells inanition."[45] Yet it is difficult to see how he can avoid becoming a department, though not necessarily a bureaucracy, and more difficult still to see what the effects would be. At the same time it is worth recalling the words of Mr. Ian Mikardo M.P. in writing about the setting up and operation of the Select Committee on Nationalised Industries: "Looking back at those early debates, I believe the chief lesson to be learned ... is the danger of prognoses about the development of political institutions. Matters seldom work out in practice as predicted. Left to themselves to find their own answers, new institutions like specialist select committees will often find their own proper place in the system and do a useful job, even if it is not the one expected of them."[46]

The third point may be simply stated. The success of an Ombudsman is likely to be greatest in the sort of political and constitutional community which needs him least. It is essentially the sort of institution which can only be effective where habits of constitutionalism are well established and are

[45] His article was entitled "An Ombudsman in Britain?"

[46] In Alfred Morris M.P. (ed.) *The Growth of Parliamentary Scrutiny by Committee*, pp. 57–58.

believed in. It is more likely to make good government better than bad government good.

Finally, I must render an account of my stewardship to Miss Hamlyn. What have I done to ensure "that the common people of the United Kingdom may realise the privileges which in law and custom they enjoy in comparison with other European peoples . . ."? So far as remedies for maladministration are concerned, it seems clear that, in some matters and through some institutions the European peoples are better off than we are. The evidence is that they have something to teach. The evidence is, also, that we are willing to learn.

INDEX